Advance Praise for *Making Waves*

"*Making Waves* is a heartfelt journey of resilience and empowerment. I was so touched by the honesty and vulnerability Helaine shared around all the challenges she faced while building her startup over a decade. This is more than a story; it's a true testament to her strength and resilience—a heartfelt narrative that will resonate with many."

—Alli Webb, Founder of Drybar

"Helaine is honest, funny, authentic, and has stories that *will* change the way you think about entrepreneurship. If you are even thinking about starting a business or a side-hustle you must read this book first."

—Vanessa Van Edwards, Bestselling Author of *Cues: Master the Secret Language of Charismatic Communication*

"For anyone that wants a demystified view of life as an entrepreneur, with extreme highs and lows, this book is for you."

—Dan Reich, 4x Exited Founder, Serial Entrepreneur, Investor, and Writer

MAKING WAVES

MAKING WAVES

HELAINE KNAPP

Post Hill
PRESS

A POST HILL PRESS BOOK
ISBN: 979-8-88845-366-7
ISBN (eBook): 979-8-88845-367-4

Post Hill Press
New York • Nashville
posthillpress.com

Published in the United States of America
1 2 3 4 5 6 7 8 9 10

TABLE OF CONTENTS

AUTHOR'S NOTE

This is not your typical hero's journey.

This is the story of how a shy, chubby girl grew into a strong, seasoned, and powerful start-up founder and executive—but the ending is far from what you might imagine.

This is about the journey, the drive, and the focus to build a massive company that would change the fitness landscape. And it's about the unlikely founder who led the charge. But it's not the rainbows and butterflies journey to get there... nor would it be at the end. Not even close.

This is my story, and I'm excited to share it with you. This was a ten-year grind, it was a tsunami of epic proportions, yet I'd do it again in a heartbeat. The deep challenges weren't the tactical elements of building, running and navigating a monster business for over ten years; instead, what wore me down was weathering the battles of start-up life that reopened the wounds of my childhood and almost broke the confidence that took years to develop.

This story is for anyone who didn't feel good enough, strong enough, skinny enough, or confident enough. It's for us, for the underdogs, the ones who started out shy and insecure and are still trying to figure out where we belong and how to navigate the world today.

It's for anyone looking to make a change, to jump into something new, who needs to dig deep to make a big decision—or learn to celebrate the small wins along the way.

You'll get a front row seat to my early years, the awkward, insecure, the anything-but-the-founder that I started out as, and what transpired and how I felt during each stepping stone that got me to the board room.

You'll learn what it was that finally got me to jump in on my own—what transpired over the prior decades to give me the confidence to actually do that. Then you'll ride the insane start-up waves with me for over a decade.

Through the good times, and the bad.

Through the big wins and epic failures.

Through a pandemic.

And through the end, which will surprise you.

This is my story—my point of view, my lens.

My lens is one through that of the founder—and you should know that founders are artists, we're never done, we're never happy, and we're always striving for more. We are both the artists of our big ideas and their biggest critic. It's a hard hat to wear (and it can be very lonely). Therefore, my vantage point throughout the story is that of the critic and seeing the tarnish: toeing the line between thinking I'm a failure and knowing I'm not. This is the story of my vision and a decade of execution. Strap in.

There's always more to the story, for book resources and more (maybe a gift!) go here: helaineknapp.com/making-waves-resources.

PROLOGUE

As I sat across the table staring at my board of directors, who stared back, some with a little sympathy, others with what looked like hatred, all I could think of was, *Haven't I been here before?*

It was the occasion of my very first board of directors meeting after my company, CITYROW, had raised our Series A round of $12 million in start-up funding.

I stood at the head of the twelve-person conference room table, rocking blue jeans (high-waisted because that's what we have to do now), a new black blazer, white t-shirt and new black booties. I had a fresh DryBar blowout, a manicure and just before the meeting started, I'd practiced my power poses in the bathroom. This was a far cry outfit wise from my Lululemon and sneakers uniform I'd been wearing for most work days over the past seven years. For today, I'd done everything I could to build up my confidence—but my hands were shaking slightly and if you listened clearly, I'm sure you could hear the tremble in my voice.

I just let the board know some bad news: we had only three months of runway left, and our growth metrics were far below our goal. I cleared my throat to deliver some more downers. I gripped the edge of the table, looking around the tiny, stuffy conference room in a midtown WeWork, wishing there was at least a window I could crack open to stop my sweating. Or maybe throw myself out of.

Around the table sat a wide range of people who were there to support the future of CITYROW. There were those I'd known for the better part of a decade, some that I'd just begun to build a relationship with, some who I had deep connections with, and others that I was almost afraid of. Some had put in large amounts of capital, some smaller, but all were meaningful. Some had been in the trenches with me solving big problems and some stood on the sidelines. Some were experts in fitness, and for some this was their first experience with franchises, hardware and connected fitness. Together, they brought a lot to the table and their job was to help guide this CITYROW ship alongside me. Technically speaking, this board is my boss.

"Now you all know there's very little left of the twelve million dollars," I said. *And you're all going to think I'm incompetent,* the little voice inside my head whispered like the devil. I still couldn't believe we were almost out of money after the largest raise we'd ever done. I was pissed… and I was pissed at myself, and scared that everyone would think me unfit to manage the company forward, despite the clear plan on how to use these funds. What had happened to the market?

The frowns of all the board members deepened.

"We executed on our big [extremely expensive] initiatives, but don't have a lot of traction, and as we all know, it's a crappy market out there, right?"

No one responded; aside from their steely glances, there was no reaction at all.

I soldiered on. "Now," I said, "We have to figure out how to reverse the company's trajectory in six weeks. And while I know the investors around the table just put capital into a recent funding round [for the second, third, even fourth time], given the market and the poor traction, we're going to need everyone in this room to put more money in immediately or the company will go under."

As I sat silently listening to the yelling and screaming around me, I floated away somewhere else, trying to drown out their fury and not internalize all that anger.

Prior to the board meeting, I'd been terrified. All this business and governance behind-the-scenes work was reaching a level of incredibly sophisticated business topics that I'd never broached. I was learning by doing and soaking up as much information from people and resources around me (like my incredible advisors and lawyers specifically). Today, instead of focusing on the concrete topics we had to handle that day and putting all my recent learnings on corporate structure and securities and fundraising options into play, I had to figure out how to navigate the wildly different people and personalities around the boardroom table and bring us all together onto the same team, the same crew.

My daydream was that I would walk out of that room with a really positive story to tell, a triumph over my very first board meeting.

Nothing of the kind happened.

And in fact, I had been here before.

Let's switch gears for a story around a different kind of table, this one in my college sorority house.

I felt like I was waiting for my execution as I sat on a small, stage-like platform in the basement of my college sorority house in front of fifty or so of my "sisters."

To be fair, my life as I knew it *did* feel like it was hanging in the balance.

To my right, Lauren was crying quietly into her hands. To my left, I could feel Jess nervously swinging her leg back and forth, and biting her thumbnail—her biggest tell that she was super stressed.

"Final agenda item," said Rachel, the sorority president, looking down at her notes. In the meeting, we had already voted on a theme for the spring formal, discussed changing our weekly chapter dinners to Tuesday nights, and nailed down a schedule for our sorority basketball team practices. I barely heard a word of anything that had been said, though, anticipating what was to come.

"Pros and Cons of Helaine, Jess, and Lauren," she said. "A reminder on how this works: everyone who wants to talk stands up and offers either a Pro or a Con for each girl. We'll tally the votes up at the end to determine their punishment—from removal from leadership positions to dismissal from the sorority."

In other words, the future of our college lives hinged on a single vote tally. And that vote would be influenced by people talking *about* us right *in front of* us. Couldn't we at least leave the room? My wildest nightmares were being realized right in front of me, in what was supposed to be a safe, supportive community that I had actually paid to be a part of.

"Helaine will be first," Rachel added.

I couldn't believe it had come to this. There in my sophomore year, I finally, *finally*, felt like I was coming into my own, after years of being a shy and quiet and chubby kid, and not really having a solid group of friends for much of my childhood and early adulthood, I'd finally found my tribe and was no longer on my own.

With the sorority, I had found my community, my friends, my people—my *sisters*. I had also started to develop my leadership chops; I had been elected social chair and into the coveted position on the sorority board.

"Pro: Helaine has been such a positive influence on me," said Tracey, a newly inducted sister, tremulously. "I wouldn't be here if it wasn't for her."

How had it all come crashing down?

During the fall rush, my crew (my pledge class) and I were in charge, responsible for running the entire recruitment process, essentially picking who would be our new sisters. And now that we knew how awesome being a part of the sorority was, we took our jobs seriously. During my entire college career, I *maybe* pulled an all-nighter or two, but during those heady weeks of rush, we never went to bed before four in the morning—this was *too* important, and we were too busy organizing the rush schedules, preparing the house and making sure every sister knew their important role to play so our house came across stunningly. We thrived on the adrenaline and excitement, not to mention the perceived seriousness of our jobs, since so far, this was the most important thing any of us had ever done!

We were insanely happy with the final set of girls on pref night—the night where you accept your bid, go to the sorority house, meet your new sisters, and toast to a future of sisterhood. Our house had been under the radar on Michigan's campus, but welcoming in our pledges—our "littles"—felt like we were ushering in a new, positive trajectory for our house.

Unlike how it happens in movies, we treated our pledges like sorority royalty, showering them with gifts, treats, and hosting them at events.

And just like that, after a few short weeks of pledging and before heading into Christmas break, it was time to initiate these new sisters—our new friends—into the house. Initiation Day was a big deal to everyone, especially those sisters who took the history, practices, and culture of our sorority to the next level. I was always excited to join a house, but for me it was about the people, the community, the support and the tribe. For others, that was part of it, but they also found excitement and connection to the history of how and why the sisterhood was built, the rules and guidelines, the doctrines and mantras. I rolled my eyes as the "prayers" we said at chapter while others embraced it like religion.

With all the littles crashing at the sorority house the night before initiation, and some older girls who lived off campus throwing a party, for some of us, it was the perfect time to celebrate in advance of the actual initiation the next day. Initiation itself was super proper: We all wore all white with strands of pearls and solemnly celebrated the super-secret rites and rituals that had been passed down from generation to generation of our sorority sisters. To college Helaine and her friends, it was time to party.

"We have to stick by the rules and bylines of this sorority," said Emily primly. "Helaine didn't do that. Con."

There were rules that came along with hanging out/living in the house, in particular, no boys or alcohol.

Those rules were broken, *often*.

That night before initiation, we pre-gamed in the house and between our friends and a big group of the littles, we *might* have been a little louder and more excited than normal. Maybe a little tipsy, too.

As we were leaving to head out to a party at some of the senior sorority sisters' houses, some of the older junior girls, our sisters, confronted us in the stairwell.

"Have you been drinking?" one of them, a tall blond with a too-tight ponytail, demanded with her arms crossed over her chest.

Of course, we were, but we weren't flaunting it, and literally everyone did it, including them.

"It's completely against the morals and standards of this sorority to drink alcohol, especially in the house," declared the tall blond, whose name was Jen. She added firmly, "Con."

While almost all our second-year friends were taken to Standards (basically an arbitrary board of sisters who reprimand you for missteps) and slapped on the wrist, three of us were singled out as the "ringleaders"—so Jess, Lauren, and I were about to be made examples of inappropriate behavior.

"This is absurd, we cannot dismiss Helaine," cried my roommate and bestie Sarah as she read the words she had written about me from a paper that shook in her hands. "Pro. Please go easy on her and take all of the amazing things she does into consideration."

Looking back with perspective, the Pro/Con vote that night wasn't just about me and my friends, it was about those sisters' need for control and authority—we were young and fun and dynamic—we were the collateral damage. As I will talk about later, nothing in life is really personal, but at the time, boy did it feel that way. It was a perfect storm of factors: probably one was about the old guard feeling jealous of our excitement to usher in a new era of the house, essentially leaving them behind, and another might have been the swell of the younger girls about to take executive positions on the board (I had just been voted social chair and our friend group made up the entire board from rush chair and finance manager to president). We were bringing new life into a previously stagnant sorority—and if there's one thing in my life I've learned, change from the old tired ways of doing things is really hard for some people to accept.

"This type of behavior really demonstrates a lack of respect for our esteemed institution," said a senior named Heather. "Con."

I couldn't help myself: I stared, boring my eyes straight into her like laser beams. I don't know how she didn't burst into flames—probably because she deliberately wouldn't make eye contact with me. I had only met her once and reminded myself that gut instincts never lie; I didn't like her then, and I don't like her now.

"Come on. We can't be hypocrites. Everyone does this. Everyone drinks in the house sometimes or gets a little rowdy," declared Nicole, the most practical and slightly nerdy member of our pledge class. "Pro."

Before the closing prayer of chapter that Sunday (being a Jew and solemnly intoning, "And so fulfills the law of Christ" every week along with the rest of the house made me giggle internally), Lauren, Jess, and I were removed from our positions on the board, but were not voted out of the house.

The little girl inside me—the former shy, chubby kid who struggles (still) with self-worth and acceptance—was both relieved but also felt like I remained on shaky ground, not to mention *fuming: Cool, enough of you like us. Thanks. I guess.*

To this day, I can still tell you the full name of every person who stood up to Pro me, and everyone who stood up to Con me. I remember the girl who would be our incoming president telling me a week later that she "politically had to Con" me because it was about upholding the rules and she wouldn't be taken seriously as the new president if she hadn't. *When people tell you who they are, believe them the first time,* I thought to myself. Despite living with her in houses for the next two years, I never trusted her again.

Tainted but not entirely down, Lauren, Jess, me, and the rest of us impacted by that night decided to stick it out with the house and the Pi Phi sisters. Though we were somewhat soured from the experience, we were still in it together and ultimately stronger and tighter for it. Isn't that what sisterhood is all about?

Years later, during my side hustling and building of my company CITYROW, I was living with the very same fellow ringleader Jess in New York City on the day I launched it. It was a fitting end to one story and beginning of another.

CHAPTER 1

A PAPER BAG OVER MY HEAD

Before I explain what actually happened in the boardroom, it's key to paint the picture of who I am both as founder of the company as well as the deeply sensitive person who eventually had to weather the perilous storms facing my start-up.

We'll start from the beginning.

Picture this: three-year-old me dressed to the nines in patent leather velcro Mary Janes, a frilly navy and white dress and dark black hair cut just above my shoulders, but with big bangs hanging down my forehead. I was holding a golf club bigger than I was with both hands over my head, red-faced with fury, stomping over to a red toy cozy coupe car, which two neighborhood boys three times my size and age were sitting in (rightfully, as it belonged to them), and ordering them out of it. They complied, I dropped the club, and got in, happily steering around our driveway, until my mom got wind of it and ran over to drag me out of the car I'd stolen.

Then imagine around the same time me sitting down with Grandma Paula who was babysitting me one afternoon.

"Gwamma," I said, taking her hand and pulling her downstairs and over to the desk where our new Apple computer sat dark. "We play the 'puda."

At a very young age, my affinity for jigsaw puzzles, which I was also doing nonstop as a kid and at which I was apparently quite advanced (although my grandma tends to be biased!), tracked with what became my long-term love of problem solving. To this day, I'm still known for pulling all-nighters to finish a good jigsaw puzzle, but really am obsessed and gravitate towards any and all kinds of puzzles. I love figuring things out. While it started with cardboard pieces of a picture, it now translates to all areas of life for me and is the foundation for one of my biggest strengths in business: creative problem solving. I'm forever questioning, curious, and strategically thinking on how to break the status quo and solve all sorts of things, which is a critical quality for someone innovating and building in business.

"Oh," Grandma said, looking at the 1988 Macintosh SE, and peering around the back to try and figure out how to turn it on, unsuccessfully. "How does it...how does it...what do we do, Helaine?"

From that day onward, my grandma took it upon herself to take computer lessons, determined to be competent alongside the future generations. For me, it was the foreshadowing of being a budding tech CEO, the start of my love and passion for technology, innovation, and games (why else would I want that computer on?!) and a natural leader that had the foresight to push into the future and bring my friends and family along for the ride (or *row*, as later became the case).

Around the same time, one of my mom's friends passed along an opportunity for me to try out to be featured as a baby model in a commercial shoot for a pasta brand, so Grandma took me to New York City for my first "audition" and press hit.

At the studio, I had to sit without her in a big room, otherwise entirely dark except for the camera shooting me. I was propped up in a high chair, with a bowl of pasta in front of me.

After forty-five minutes of me staring at the pasta and wondering where I was, where my grandma was, and why there was brown mush in front of me (this was the eighties; whole wheat pasta was new), they pushed me. "Helaine, just taste it," the producer kept saying to me over and over again.

"No more," I finally declared.

"Please taste it now," the producer snapped.

So, as the budding people pleaser I was becoming, I took a quick bite. Then I dumped the entire bowl of pasta on the floor before I smiled up at him. To his eyes, it probably looked like a problem child at her finest—but I still ended up getting the gig because I was the only little kid auditioning who didn't cry. My family loves telling this story, perhaps because it became a great print ad of me as a cute kid and a fond memory of me and my grandma. However, it's also a great early example of what would become an early lesson in what to expect in business: Sometimes, you may want to cry, but you just need to sit down, show up, and do your job. There would be hundreds of times in my future career where all I wanted to do was cry and throw the proverbial pasta on the floor. Sometimes I channel that inner childhood strength and hold in the tears (a key skill I've developed) and sometimes, more often than I'd like to admit, I'm just human. The emotions take over, and I don't show up maturely, instead giving in and throwing whatever is bugging me right on the floor.

These childhood stories are examples of the truest me: bossy and brassy and sure of herself in every way—before the outside world influenced me too much. In my rawest form, I was precocious as hell.

I was also determined and strong, sometimes to a fault. When I was eleven, Grandpa started teaching me to play golf. As directed, I took his three wood and continued hitting the ball and hitting the ball and hitting the ball. I was precocious but also exacting—hard on myself (so was he)—and always wanted to get things right out of the gate. I was focused and wanted to be the best.

Suddenly, I hit the golf ball. And the ground. I hit it so hard that the head of the club just broke off. I'm not sure how easy it is to break a titanium golf club (I have yet to do this since and can hang decently for nine holes of golf), but I *am* sure I'm very strong and determined, and the broken golf club was collateral damage that day.

Alongside this kind of strength, I'm also a deeply sensitive creature. One day when I was around eleven, I was dressed in my workout / biking gear in all my 90's kid glory, driving with my mom to go on a bike ride. As I was sitting in the back seat taking in the normal scenery of my childhood neighborhood, I looked out the window and suddenly shrieked, "Mom!!!"

Mom slammed on the brakes with her hand on her heart, and looked back at me, alarmed.

"What is it, Helaine?" she asked.

"Look," I said, pointing out the window at a car pulled over to the side of the road, its hazards on and a police car pulled up behind it, lights flashing. "Someone needs help. Can you pull over so we can help them?"

"Honey," my mom said, resuming driving and looking at me in the rearview mirror while I craned my neck to watch the pulled-over car worriedly. "The police will help that person. We don't need to pull over."

But it was hot, we had a carful of water, and eventually she caved. We stopped and ended up sharing some of the water from our upcoming bike ride with the people whose car had broken down. My sensitive and empathetic self always wants to help people, which sometimes creates a dichotomy or paradox for me as a powerful executive. Over time, I've learned to channel that empathy and eventually to lead with it.

There was also the me who wore a paper bag over my head (something I wanted to do many times as an adult but that's a story for later). One evening when I was around ten years old, my mom and her friend Judy were sitting at the white Formica table in our kitchen.

I came into the room *wearing a paper grocery bag firmly over my head* to get a juice box out of the fridge. I was so shy I couldn't handle the prospect of connecting with Judy, even though I'd grown up with her kids and knew her extremely well.

Golf club attacks notwithstanding, I was and am a sweet and deeply sensitive and empathetic human being, outwardly bold but also introspective, internal, and at times introverted.

As with many women, something happened along the way to quell my voice and my verve. By third grade, I remember being conscious of being chubby, and not being cool. I can still vividly picture the lunchroom table I was sitting at—black Formica, peeling at the edges—when Nate, a cute boy a grade above me, approached.

"Hey," he said. I couldn't believe my luck that he wanted to talk to me.

"Hey," I replied, playing it cool. (I guarantee you it wasn't cool).

"I saw you downstairs after the physical," he said. My stomach dropped a little.

"Mmm hmmm," I said noncommittally.

"How much did you weigh?" he asked.

"Um, I can't remember," I said, trying to be quiet so no one else around us heard the conversation. But of course, they were all listening.

"I can!" he crowed. "You weigh seventy-five pounds! That's *fifteen pounds* heavier than me!"

By that point, I was tall, shy, and chubby—increasingly uncomfortable in my own skin—and, no shocker, desperate to fit in, and that conversation with Nate did me no favors. And considering I can remember and feel it twenty-something years later, I'd say it left its mark.

In retrospect, I sometimes didn't do myself any favors, either. Like that one time in elementary school when I chose the double bass as my preferred musical instrument. I picked it precisely because it looked like a challenge I could conquer (hello, foreshadowing), but at age ten, it was social suicide.

❧

And then there was summer camp. (I recognize that I was far more fortunate than many others to have the opportunity to go to summer camp and enjoy many other activities with my family). You know how in the movies, it's either an idyllic time where people find their first love and lifetime friends, or it's a setting in a horror movie where a bunch of people end up dead by some crazed killer. Well, my experience wasn't *quite* that bad...but it wasn't great.

Here's the thing: my entire family *loved* camp, both the idea and the practice of it. My grandmother met her first husband at camp. My mom loved camp from the age of six. My dad went for ten years, refusing to leave until he was already in law school and had done five years as the waterfront director after being a camper.

So, they picked an amazing over-the-top camp for me, literally the most luxurious, gorgeous place ever in Maine. There were activities every night, scavenger hunts, going off-campus, climbing the wall, going swimming every day, waterskiing, everything. I *love* activities, so it was mind-blowing for nine-year-old me.

But at the end of the day, I still didn't fit in.

And then my grandma stepped in. She loved spoiling me since day one, and camp—care packages!—was no different. Grandma also loves fashion, and I think that she wanted to make sure that her granddaughter was well represented at camp.

So, she sent me a package of the Michael Stars t-shirts, size XL—literally one in every color—as an attempt to help me fit into the fanciest camp out there, but of course it didn't help.

I was quite simply an outcast, and girls were as mean as they get at that age. No matter how nice or perfectly on-trend of an outfit I wore, I still stood out in all the wrong ways, and that didn't change anything.

I had some friends, but I never fully felt like I belonged. While the camp was idyllic, perfect in activities any kid would dream of having, it was tainted with a sense that I was only there on the surface, never really cracking into the deep friendships that people love about camp in books or movies. I wanted to be someone who loved camp and whom camp loved. But at that place and time, it just wasn't a good fit.

In retrospect, the idea of camp for me was probably tied in part to my family legacy and their deep love of camp for generations. It was also a place of hope that because of the epic success among other members of my family, it is where I'd maybe finally fit in. When I didn't, it hit harder. I felt a big disappointment in myself that I wasn't able to thrive in the same way generations of my family did, at least in the stories I'd heard growing up. I wanted what they all had and didn't get that at all. It took me years to accept that it was time to move on.

I'm resilient, though, so back then I never gave up. I'd leave camp at the end of August and by the time it rolled around to re-enroll in January, I'd forgotten the bad parts and decided to try one more time ... I ended going back *five* times, each summer more determined than the one before that I'd crack open and make those lifelong friends/find the belonging. Ultimately, I found other outlets with a better group of friends to connect with later on, but it's still sad to think about that period, because there's a part of me that knows I'd really thrive at camp. It's like a retroactive FOMO, but also the fact that I kept going back, pushing myself to fit in and make it work, is a clear sign of my future stubbornness and resilience.

Without friends, I became besties with the counselors. Honestly, they were more interesting and they could tame my frizzy long hair into polished braids. Best of all, they were nice to me. Looking back, I was always mature beyond my years. I didn't quite (yet) fit in anywhere, but like many of us, I knew I had something in me and that one day it would shine through. I spent a lot of those early years watching and listening—and with such deep sensitivity, I (unfortunately or fortunately) always knew when someone was talking about me, especially in a negative way. This ended up making me the sharp observer of human nature I've become as an adult. It is something that has served me in every way, especially in business, because fundamentally, business is understanding and working with people in intuitive (and productive) ways.

Later in high school, I'd find my niche in a different youth group camp my mother forced me to go to. There I found my tribe of like-minded chill humans who saw me and loved me for who I was and that environment started to nurture back out the charismatic leader that had been shut in for so many years. This community was where I ran for an office for the first time—first as local chapter president and then as regional VP—and won (many times over), stepping onto a cornerstone of acceptance and freedom that was in turn the stepping stone to my personal development and coming out of my shell in college and beyond.

Even as I was growing up and starting to bust out, though, the hits kept coming, even from people close to me.

During a family party, I was chatting with my grandpa, whom I'd always loved and admired. We were very close and I saw him and my grandmother weekly, as they came to our sports games and babysat us regularly. We visited them in Florida in the winters, learned all their favorite sports and games like golf, tennis, backgammon, and cards.

He was so excited when I told him I'd gotten accepted into the University of Michigan—his first wife had gone there and he'd always loved the institution. He immediately started making plans—that night!—to take me out to dinner with the whole family at a fancy restaurant to celebrate. Grandpa was a very prim and proper wealthy man and all I could remember thinking when he mentioned that dinner was, "Shit, now I'm going to have to blow dry my hair." He liked women to be put together and polished at all times and I was still mastering my mane of curls.

A few weeks before I left for college he asked to take me on a walk around our local lake. I obliged because I was always excited to spend some one-on-one time with either of my grandparents.

Before I left, I showered, straightened my hair (he wasn't shy about preferring it straight to the curls that had found their way to my head during my early teens) and put on a chic outfit that my style maven grandmother had bought for me. At the meeting spot in between our houses, we had parked our cars, started walking around the lake and were talking about the upcoming plan to drive to Michigan, what I would need for the dorm room, when they would come and visit.

Then he paused, mid-conversation.

"You know, Helaine…," he started.

I looked at him with wide eyes and a big smile, ready to embrace whatever life wisdom he was about to impart. I knew it was going to be really good.

"…You're really going to have to lose weight if you ever want to find a husband."

I don't remember a single other word from that conversation, which carried on for a while longer. My seventeen-year-old self cried inside but couldn't cry on the outside, because I couldn't let him know how badly and deeply he had hurt me. In our family, we were strong and powered through, so I swallowed my tears. I've never forgotten those words, though, even all these years later, when I'm fit and very husband-worthy, on my own terms.

Despite this incident, my grandpa was wonderful and the person I'd think of most as I built CITYROW. I know he would've been beaming with pride to watch me side-hustle my way into the founding and CEO-ship of CITYROW. He was an entrepreneur himself and would have gotten such a kick out of this journey I'd embarked on. In fact, back when I was in high school, in a moment of pure prescience, he cut out an article in the *New York Times* about how women should row for physical and mental health, and mailed the newspaper clipping to me, saying, "Rowing seems great for camaraderie and social stuff, plus you're strong and you have the stamina, so you should try it."

Like every other human, everything I experienced impacted me, the good, the bad, even the neutral. The way I carried myself early on—and especially being overweight growing up—had a huge impact on me, and bubbled right back to the surface many years later, even after I had shed the top layer of the overweight double bass player, when I started CITYROW and became a mogul in the fitness space.

Over the years, my strong personality was both a real blessing and sometimes a curse, or at least off-putting. My big personality showed itself before almost anything else—I was a *lot* as a kid, as you saw—and then the silencing for a stretch was real.

I often felt untethered. I was born as an empath and then based on my experiences growing up, especially when I felt like an outsider, I heightened those abilities to learn to know what other people needed, wanted, and expected. This was painful to experience but also the foundation for my superpowers later in life. I found a really good outlet for that major part of me in my work and in the business. Now, I embrace being bossy and prescriptive—those things are huge assets as long as you're doing them in an effective way—with strong listening skills to complement! So, I like to think I figured out a way to challenge the silencing—or maybe channel it is a better word—and grow into having the strong-ass voice I have today.

CHAPTER 2

PROS AND CONS

The infamous night of Pros and Cons in my sorority house put a finer point on who I was becoming as a person, but my college years were so incredibly formative, chock full of experiences that continued to shape who I am as a person, a friend, a businesswoman, and a daughter.

It was a time for personal growth, but also fun, and let's say, perhaps, not the vision of health and wellness I would later embody (three-story beer bongs, late night nachos, and dining hall eating left their mark, but it was also hella fun and I'm so grateful to have had four incredible years in Ann Arbor.).

Enmeshed in all of it was sorority rush, something I'd been really looking forward to. Part of my decision to go to Michigan was that I'd always wanted to join Greek life. I was excited for community, comradery, and to be part of something bigger than me, something I'd been missing growing up and never got at summer camp. We're all looking for belonging and connection, and at eighteen, I was no different. In fact, I probably needed it more than others and genuinely thought it was my chance to find my crew.

I wanted a cool Jewish-centric house—certainly some kind of camp redemption now that I knew I'd come out of my shell and was generally awesome—and I narrowed it down to three or four houses that felt right to me and that I could aspire to belong to.

Rush started the second week of school. It was tightly organized and exhausting; you'd head like soldiers to the Student Union, get a schedule of what houses you were scheduled to visit, and then you'd get to one of them and line up with a bunch of other hopefuls. You'd be ushered in and paired with a sister to sit on the floor and have a chat, then move around to talk to two or three more. You were trying to be cool and impressive, but also knew they were judging you. Not hypothetically; that was literally their job. This process brought out all my insecurities from being a chubby kid and outsider to suppressing my big personality and sense of humor.

After each "round," you'd go back to the Student Union and rank your preferences. The sororities would rank you too, then you'd see which ones you matched with.

I had very few callbacks and almost pulled out entirely from the process. I cried a lot, particularly because acquaintances of mine happened to know people in houses who were older and influential and that was definitely a factor in them getting chosen. I didn't have those ties and was frustrated; I knew this process wasn't doing my personality justice. Maybe I should have tried harder at camp, then I'd know older girls in the houses? I'm also sure many of the women in different houses judged me for being chubby, plus I was also still coming out of my shell, so I felt insecure and intimidated and nervous. At the time, the process was not conducive to anyone with an ounce of shyness or insecurity, and while I like to think I'd show up better today, the rush pressure-cooker got the best of me then.

I almost didn't go to the final pref night but for some reason, a few conversations I'd had with the women at the sorority that I ended up joining kept repeating in my mind, and that stuck out for me as a reason to go back, despite that house being *so* wildly differently from what I'd probably been dreaming about since signing on to attend Michigan.

On pref night, I remember wearing sunglasses inside, even after the sun went down. I wasn't happy to be there and I was deeply emotional and disappointed. Despite my best efforts, the tears flowed. My Big Sister would later tell me she told people there was no way I was joining their house because I'd been so upset! That probably didn't make the best impression, but between the tears that night, I also met some other girls who would be in my pledge class. That ended up being the most important factor—that I liked my cohort—so I decided to give that sorority a shot.

That period, like for most people who get the opportunity to live away from home for the first time, was pivotal in teaching me to navigate different worlds, especially my internal one, learning to adapt to almost anything thrown my way, people and situations alike. I became a chameleon of sorts, making it all begin to work for me.

As mentioned, college definitely held one of the first public blows in my life when my sorority debated (in front of me) whether I should stay in the house. I witnessed sisters stand up and say why I should stay or leave, and then, when enough people voted to keep me, I weathered that shit storm and came out stronger. In retrospect, like so many things, this was a time that felt very dark—painful and unfair—and yet I bounced back and found my strong and confident place as a respected leader in the sorority. I led us in triumph as captain of our house during Greek Week; we came in third after not placing for decades. That was a first major showcase of my leadership, creativity, and organizational skills... and I felt like I was finally in the right seat.

The trauma I went through the year prior—the trial and the sentencing—and the fact that I persevered and stuck around (for myself and my sisters) actually pushed me further along in my leadership. I was knocked down but wasn't out; I started tapping into my quiet confidence and gained the respect of others around me.

～

Before I almost drowned in the perils of start-up life I was once actually lost at sea, for a few hours.

We were on a big family vacation in Turks and Caicos, and on the fourth day I, along with my cousins Jake and Rebecca and my aunt Amy, decided to do a jet skiing adventure on the other side of the island. We were told where we could go—not very far to the left, but we could go all the way to the right where there are little inlets. Beyond two of the inlets, we would see Emerald Cay, the $35-million home famous on the island. We could go all the way out to the end of the rocks, then no further. It was almost four thirty in the afternoon and we had an hour out on the water. Jake and I hopped on our jet skis speeding to the right together as Aunt Amy and Rebecca took off slowly to the left.

We rode fast, Jake creating huge wakes, and kept on going. A bit later, we realized it was already past five in the afternoon and we thought we should head back in, as the sun was already beginning to go down.

We had paused to take a picture, so we turned our jet skis off. Once we were done, I tried turning on my jet ski. Nothing happened. I turned the key this way and that, fiddled with the engine, but nothing worked. Jake tried too, to no avail. The waves were huge, and with my jet ski dead, it suddenly capsized, I was thrown into the water. We got back on Jake's jet ski and tried looping a rope around the steering of the dead jet ski to tow it but it capsized again. As if things weren't already awesome, the engine cracked from the rough waters. Jake and I stayed on the one jet ski, but could only move about an inch at a time to avoid capsizing yet again. We went from speed demons to being the slowest people ever on a jet ski.

At half past five, we had a beautiful sunset to watch. The dark was creeping in quickly, though.

"I think we should head towards shore then eventually get off the jet skis while there's any light so we can find a good place to land," Jake called over his shoulder.

"No way!" I screamed. "We're not getting off this jet ski! There are probably sharks circling us right now! They probably already sent the boat out to rescue us but they'll never find us on that massive and remote part of the island!"

Fifteen more minutes passed and the sun was now completely down, the stars starting to come out along with the glow worms in the water. Jake and I looked at the constellations for a while, then we both started to freak out. Where was the rescue boat? I'd seen the movie *Open Water*. I know what happens to forgotten people on vacation. I really hoped no one told Grandma we were missing, but we'd clearly already missed dinner and our overbearing Jewish family had to be freaking out.

We were both shivering at this point.

At a quarter to seven, we were still idling forward—in the inky black night—and making progress; not a lot, but some.

I was *really* starting to get scared and yet I fought back tears because I knew crying would just make things worse. I forced myself to stay calm. Also, where the hell was that rescue boat?

Finally, we could see that enormous Emerald Cay estate in the distance.

"Jake," I said, pointing. "We're going there."

"No!" He screamed. I think he was starting to lose it a little. "What are you going to do, trespass? What if they're not home? We should reconsider just docking on this land."

I ignored him and invoked the "older cousin" doctrine—we were going to Emerald Cay, whether he liked it or not.

We'd been on a jet ski for almost three hours, it was nighttime, and I knew people were worried about us. Please arrest me for trespassing, let that be my only problem.

There wasn't a dock, but we managed to find a semi-shallow area, and I jumped off, climbed over the rocks, and clambered onto a pathway. Jake wouldn't leave the jet skis so I told him to wait in the gazebo and I would go find help.

As I walked around the outside of this massive house, I started sobbing, complete Helaine hysterics (that I'd been trained to keep suppressed but sometimes come out at all the wrong times), from the relief of being on land and so close to being rescued, I hoped. The place was so big and magnificent it took me a good five minutes to find the front door; there was no doorbell and the door was literally too thick to knock on, but I saw the lights from a TV flickering somewhere and just started banging and screaming hello. I kept screaming. Finally, a man holding a baby came to the door. I was still in such hysterics, at this point from clear relief, knowing we were okay and on land. My thoughts and worries now turned toward my family who was certainly freaking out, and I couldn't stop the tears. The man asked me to come in, but I told him I needed to find Jake, at a gazebo out there somewhere.

"Which gazebo?" he asked calmly.

We went and got Jake and the man welcomed us inside. After we each chugged two bottles of water, I told him we were staying at the Veranda Hotel and could we please call our family, knowing they would by now be absolutely frantic.

Fifteen-year-old Jake, now feeling safe, calmly asked for a tour as if this was just another stop on our family vacation. I, on the other hand, was on a mission to contact our family and let them know we were safe. Now that I knew I was okay, I was freaking out that *they* were freaking out.

Our hotel was brand new and wasn't yet in the phone book (the estate had no internet, don't ask me why), so I called the established hotel next door to the Veranda and made them Google the number. For me, it was a sign of my ability to be a great creative problem-solver and navigate tricky situations with unique solutions, even amidst my tears and fears.

We finally got back to the hotel, greeted by twenty-five staff members and my sobbing parents. Everyone at the hotel hugged us and were minor celebrities for the rest of our stay.

This story at the end of college as I prepared to enter the real working world might just be the beginning of me stepping back into my power—owning my strengths and embracing my truest self, which looks a lot like that three-year-old me: smart, savvy, and resilient—and maybe a little bossy. Good instincts not to go on land, but to find the house; not afraid of breaking some rules (light trespassing); breaking down when I was overwhelmed but then staying calm and strong for my family (and later, my team). Resilience. Strong survival instincts. Making the best of the worst situation. Betting on me. Knowing it would work out.

CHAPTER 3

FROM HUSTLE TO FLOW

*I*t's an unpopular opinion, but everyone should start at the bottom. Most people get out of school having done well and expect to slide right into that senior role with cool projects, perks, and control. I get it, it's more fun, but you miss out on building your business foundation.

The summer between junior and senior years at Michigan, I walked into the vaunted doors of 4 Times Square—the legendary Condé Nast building in New York City—to start working at *Cookie*, a now-folded magazine for rich young parents highlighting and helping them source expensive items and services for their kids and homes. Yes, that shy, chubby kid you've been hearing all about was now officially an infamous Condé Nast intern (it's all about who you know, and my mom's best friend Andrea decided this was going to be my job and worked her own magic to make it happen!).

Out of the gates, I was excellent at working, at being an intern, at getting things done. I loved emails, I loved tasks, I loved being busy and crushing to-do lists. I loved the buzzy office environment, the people, the politics, and being good at something. It surprised me how much I loved it and how much it felt like I had found my place: it awoke something in me.

I did so much work on a daily and weekly basis, and kept asking for more, that my *Cookie* bosses started handing me any and everything they could to satiate my hunger for accomplishing tasks and becoming an integral part of the team. At the time, I equated performance to speed and volume of tasks, and boy did I deliver. Before long, I blew through the classic intern work. I remember the day they handed me a big, black, three-inch binder and instructed me how to process invoices (usually reserved for a higher-level person in the Finance department with an MBA). This kept me busy but also left me wanting even more.

It wasn't just in my head; I did well and clearly added value so much that they asked me back (yup, they preemptively asked an intern to return). So the following summer, I found myself striding back through the massive glass doors of 4 Times Square once again. That year, though, rather than sharing a cubicle with other interns, I had my own office. This "office" was actually a rickety makeshift desk stationed *inside* the merch closet—but it was mine and despite the lack of windows, I had my own door, so in my mind, I'd made it. Given my proximity to the merch, I became in charge of doling out and managing back issues of the magazines alongside endless numbers of cheeky promotional merchandise including onesies saying "Tough Cookie," "Smart Cookie," and "Cool Cookie." Weirdly, I felt right at home.

My responsibilities suddenly and unexpectedly blossomed into me having to make calls for the marketing team, as in, using the telephone to talk to strangers. The first few times I did it, I actually cried (a recurring theme if you haven't noticed).

I'd like to point out that in these calls I was so terrified to make, I wasn't even trying to get people to buy something. I was calling to tell people they'd *won a sweepstakes*: they literally could not have been better calls to be making, but yet, they paralyzed me. Even after everything that I'd been through (and grown into) during those college years and into young adulthood, I was still a shy and insecure kid on the inside. The calls were going outside my comfort zone—in a big way!

The only option I had was to power through this challenge I faced, so I did, dozens of times over, eventually feeling so comfortable on the phone that I asked for more tasks in that realm, offering to call any and everyone, and the skill has stuck—to this day I'm never afraid to use my texting device to make phone calls, although not all of my friends are thrilled by this.

Somewhere along the way, my bosses sensed the leader in me—either that, or they just really needed someone to manage the plethora of other interns—a.k.a., the kids of important Condé Nast clients that nobody could say no to hiring—and they put me in charge. I was officially the boss for the very first time…to a bunch of other not-quite-as-eager eighteen- and nineteen-year-olds, maybe six to twelve months younger than me.

Despite my eagerness to please and excel, I made so many mistakes.

To start, my new vaunted position went right to, and stayed in, my head to the point where I walked around the office, "correcting" (that is, bossing) my charges when I didn't even have to, or for the tiniest thing. They'd ask me if they were doing something right, and even if it was totally fine, I felt like I had to exert my superiority over them and make some kind of light correction or change. I kept all the good, visible work for myself and probably more than once took a little too much credit myself for the entire team's work. I cringe hard now thinking about how I handled those early days.

One day, the associate editor called me into her office. I practically skipped into her plush space, already imagining the praise that was about to be heaped on me for a job well done.

"Helaine," she said sternly, looking up from a preview of our upcoming issue, not offering me a seat. "You need to stop bossing the other interns around. It's obnoxious and you're intimidating them."

I'd assumed I was getting another set of positive affirmations, but instead I got a talking-to and walked out of there more than a little red-faced. I'd made my first mistake in management, yet even that couldn't quell my enthusiasm for this working environment and being a boss.

After two intern summers under my belt, I got my first "real" job in September 2008 (sliding in just under the financial crash of that year and the next) as a sales assistant at *W* magazine.

I immediately made sure I was an integral part of the team, even as a low level sales assistant. I quickly rose to being the most competent, going above and beyond and after a few short months, was the assistant whom all the reps would fight over. I also managed the internal politics of being a team member; that is, being the last one standing at the company holiday party and first in the office the next day to prove a different kind of point. I'd like to thank my four years in Ann Arbor for building that skill set.

Sometimes, my hyper-competence—and realization that not everyone else was like me—got the best of me. I made more mistakes. I walked into *W* humble and excited, but it became apparent pretty quickly that I was wildly overqualified for the position of a sales assistant. In maybe three months max, I'd mastered my craft and started to think about how to take the job to the next level without being asked (I'd heard that was a good thing to do in the working world).

I did things like figure out how to work the back-end system that logged all the magazines. It was this weird, archaic program that was all black and white digits—it wasn't remotely intuitive—but my puzzle-building skills came in handy and I quickly learned the tech to be able to search the archives of the magazines to help my bosses and make their jobs infinitely easier.

But then I also started to get a little too confident that I was God's gift to sales assistant-dom. I got frustrated when I realized that people weren't as competent as I was. For example, my boss Jane, whom I loved, and who treated me well, sat near me. She couldn't hack anything at all in Excel, which was a pretty important part of our jobs, and I had to teach her over and over.

Finally, one day I snapped tartly, "Jane, I've been going over this with you for weeks. You *need* to figure it out."

Without a word, Jane got up, took my arm, and pulled me into a nearby conference room and sat me down, immediately reminding me of when I'd gotten yelled at for over-managing the interns at *Cookie*.

She gave me hell for speaking to her that way, in front of other colleagues no less, and put me right back in my place. She was right and it was a great early lesson in respect. Of course, in the moment, I immediately burst into my default—tears (if you've learned anything at this point about me, it's that I cry, often). Outside of a strong lesson in respect and hierarchy, I realized part of my value was in complementing the skill sets of others on the team, even my boss. Not everyone shares the same skill sets as you do and that you can't be mad at them for that. In fact, we have to work with all kinds of people, and ideally meet them where they're at, not where we think they should be. This misstep was so valuable it paved the way for a foundation of understanding and respecting structures and to keep any/all frustration at bay—passive aggressiveness has no place in the working world.

❧

After mastering the craft of being a sales assistant, and hungry for more and a faster pace, a friend of a friend helped me land a job at the tech start-up Buddy Media. It was a booming social media marketing tech company thriving in the world of helping brands understand and build on social media. We were a software as a service (SaaS) company and agency, and the game was constantly changing as the world of social media was, at that time, directly on the fast track. This was in 2010 and Facebook was at its peak, just starting to let brands onto the platform. It was the wild, wild west for social media.

At Buddy Media, I quickly learned the trade of being a great project manager, became an onboarding trainer for new hires, and started being given top accounts based on my reputation for account management. Once again, I thrived on being successful. I like being good at things and knew I was good at the world of work, so the more and bigger I could do it, the more something seemed like a challenge, a puzzle, or an adventure, the more I wanted to sign up for it. Growing up, I was decent at sports, horrible at art and music, and fine at school, but never excelled in any of those areas. Here, working, hustling, and navigating people and projects, I settled into my place in the world, and it was so much fun.

Buddy Media was a big step up—not only did I actually get to talk to the clients at this company, but I was also managing them. There were endless opportunities to grow, something I was keen on and excited to excel at. It also meant more was at stake and there were more opportunities to fumble.

The company, less than eighty people when I started, grew quickly to almost two hundred people, and we were outgrowing our three floors on West 31st Street. We had been told we'd soon move into a new office down on Spring Street and we were all excited for the Soho digs. One day, about a year into my tenure there, I was told our team was being moved to that new office about three months before the rest of the company officially did.

When I heard the news from my boss in a team meeting, I had an immediate visceral reaction and got upset. As someone who typically has very big energy in any given situation, for me to go suddenly silent and be very clearly bothered affected the whole room. The maturity beyond my years left me and I acted like the young twenty-three-year-old I was at the time.

It was a completely short-sighted reaction, but it also represented exactly how I felt and that young twenty-three-year-old me was here to win, and that this move somehow threatened my position or was going to affect my status in the company because I wasn't going to be in the line of sight of the executive team every day. I had come to thrive on that visibility and, if I'm being honest, the validation that came with it. I was determined to grow at the company and I liked that everyone could see me front and center. It was where I shined: I got to talk to everyone, make great impressions, and develop strong contacts. I also liked being seen at the office working late—another notch on my success belt (though I disagree with this type of value in today's world). Instead, now I had to work from a satellite office for a couple of months without seeing the rest of the company. After the news broke, I sat at my desk and stifled tears.

In retrospect, the move was a huge compliment to our team and my boss at the time—the higher-ups respected our team to not slack off by being less supervised because we were that capable and mature (ahem, or trying to be).

There were obviously some ups and downs as I grew into myself, especially professionally, but I would not trade these early and lower-level jobs for anything. They set the foundation, they built my grit, they put me in my place, and they taught me more than I'd ever imagined. Occasional brattiness aside, these critical experiences taught me the interpersonal relations that are foundational to both the politics of life in general and specifically those in business. Sitting in those seats taught me how to anticipate people's needs, how to understand my place in the ecosystem, and how to get creative about how I could move up and be a little bit more visible.

It's an unpopular opinion, but everyone should start at the bottom. Most people get out of school having done well and expect to slide right into that senior role with cool projects, perks, and control. I get it, it's more fun, but you miss out on building your business foundation.

I wouldn't be successful if it wasn't for those internships and early career days riding the lowest rung on the ladder. When you're at the bottom, you see things very differently, have a specific vantage point, and gain a more holistic world view. It ultimately makes you stronger as you grow. Chances are, *Cookie* magazine's intern me would roll my eyes at this, but at minimum, I think people should have to wear every hat. Value is in the perspective and if you ultimately want to wear—and succeed at wearing—a *bigger* hat, you will be better at that role having tried them all, especially the smallest one.

Learning those lessons early on were critical later as I navigated unbelievable interpersonal dynamics at CITYROW with a powerful board of directors and investors, some of whom gave me hell and with whom I often went head-to-head with. The hits kept and always do keep coming, but I know my early days gave me the strong foundation for understanding people and business dynamics, without which I would've been even more lost later on in dealing with things that were so much harder and more complicated than I could have ever imagined.

CHAPTER 4

HOW IS MY BACK BROKEN?

F ast forward a couple of years.

One miserable February day in 2014, during a huge snowstorm, I found myself lying in a room of the Hospital for Special Surgery breathing heavily, trying to will away the agony in my back. It had been a long morning and I was in so much pain that I couldn't even lift my leg—my dad and two orderlies had to lift me onto the gurney when we arrived.

I lay awkwardly on the exam table on my left side with my legs extended at a 110-degree angle, the only position I'd found to be mildly bearable.

"Look at her," the top surgeon at HSS said to my parents. "There's no way we can send her home like this. She needs surgery *right now*. It's my day off, but we're going to get an OR and do this today."

Surgery was the thing we'd been avoiding for two years. Since my lower back started to hurt chronically, I'd tried everything: meditation, stretching, physical therapy, back braces, manifesting being pain-free, yoga, even rounds and rounds of steroids and epidurals. Nothing worked. Then, two weeks before, I casually moved in a way that took me to a new level of pain—and it had gotten steadily worse over the next two weeks to the point that I could barely get up to go to the bathroom. I finally (and reluctantly) made it clear to my parents how bad it was and they came into the city to take care of me and make plans.

That next morning, which happened to be Valentine's Day, I woke up with my parents as my roommates. I'd relinquished all control, accepted all the help (two things I acknowledge aren't my favorite things but I'm working on!) and six hours later, I went in for the emergency back surgery. In the middle of a snowstorm. With no health insurance. Let one major lesson of this book be to always have active health insurance, either immediately setting it up through a new provider or by activating COBRA. The second lesson is that most of the time there is a grace period to retroactively enact said health insurance, thankfully. And luckily, there is no one better at navigating a tough phone call than my mom, who by the time I went in for the surgery itself, had it all figured out.

As I lay on the operating table about to go under, still feeling like someone had stabbed me in the hip and dragged the dagger down to my foot, all my experiences and adventures and life lessons running at warp speed through my head, my last thought before I drifted off was, *How did I get here?*

Buddy Media sold to Salesforce.com for just under $1 billion in 2012, the second largest tech "exit" in NYC at the time. It was exciting, to say the least. I had been at Buddy Media for just under two years but in that time, I'd grown as a person, made new friends (my work friends from this time are some of my strongest relationships to date), and excelled at many jobs within Buddy Media. I was in a sales account management role by the time we found our new home at Salesforce. As with most transitions, the new job was fine, but I essentially went from running my own book of business (some of the most prominent and top accounts at Buddy Media) to working for the Salesforce sales reps, essentially doing their paperwork. I knew it wasn't a good fit and neither did a mentor friend of mine who told me he'd found the perfect new place for me.

In October 2012, right after the city cleaned up from Hurricane Sandy, I started as the sixth employee at Olapic, a hot new SaaS tech company helping brands leverage the power of user-generated content to drive e-commerce performance. I was brought on to build and run the Client Services team. I was ready to be part of something new from the ground up, get my hands dirty, and really test my leadership and sales skills.

It was right around then that my back first started feeling wonky, so I started popping Advil multiple times per day, then going to physical therapy, getting MRIs, getting steroid injections via epidural, and eventually, even wearing a back brace. Nothing helped much.

That was a few years into me falling fast and hard for the boutique fitness scene in NYC, which was absolutely booming. SoulCycle had led the charge a few years prior, the founders growing their multimillion-dollar business by handing out flyers themselves on the West Side Highway to runners and bikers to advertise their lone rinky-dink studio on the Upper West Side, and suddenly boutique fitness studios were a *thing*—and I was in it to win it.

My love of boutique fitness came naturally as part of a wellness journey I'd been on since the end of college and really picked up steam in my first few years navigating NYC as a young professional when I was at Buddy Media. As a heavier-set kid growing up, my family spent countless hours and dollars trying to get me to lose weight, but it wasn't until senior year that I started to make moves on my own. First with a trainer off campus (Bally Total Fitness FTW) and then with my college friends, who encouraged week-end nights in, to cook healthy dinners versus going out and pound-ing as many drinks as we could before a late-night nacho binge.

This continued as I moved into my first apartment in NYC with my three best friends from high school—four girls and one bathroom where you had to open the dishwasher to open the oven! We supported each other in healthy habits, going to the gym, and cooking healthy dinners. That first gym I belonged to in NYC's Stuyvesant Town, where we lived, was the first actual com-munity fitness I found. After tackling the machines on my own, and dabbling with getting a trainer, I started taking the kickboxing and then spin classes they offered in the two rooms in the back of the tiny space. Don kicked my ass in kickboxing—I still remember the gross feeling of having to put those nasty and sweaty (not to mention smelly) gloves on, but it was fun and challenging to crush a left-right-hook-uppercut combo ten times over. Carter took me through my first, then countless, spin class, and before long I was a regular and familiar face among the community. That, coupled with a strong commitment to WeightWatchers (in person meet-ings were clutch, within StuyTown and even overlapping with my gym buddies), and the weight started to really come off. Before long, I vowed never to see my highest number on the scale again and learned healthy habits and a relationship to food that has stuck with me to this day.

People started noticing. At first, I hated the comments from my friends, family, my friends' parents, literally anyone who'd known me "before." It felt awkward to hear them comment on my body—even if it was a compliment. It certainly helped increase my confidence and self-esteem and I eventually got over the awkwardness because it was something I was doing for myself. It was an investment in me and I was incredibly proud of myself. Also, I crushed the WeightWatchers points paradigm, just one more example of how much I love points and games…and winning. There wasn't any one big event to spark my weight loss, I think it was just about when I was ready. No number of external factors could fuel (or detract from) that intrinsic drive. Everything happens in the time that it should, in life and business, and everything in between.

It was a constant choice between living the life of a young professional in NYC and going out with co-workers for happy hour, burgers, pizza, or going home and going to the gym, but I made enough consistently good choices, and they paid off. However, as I grew in my professional career, it became harder to say no to the client dinner, make it to the gym classes at six thirty, or even drop my stuff at home and take myself there for a workout when I wasn't leaving my desk until eight at night.

Just around the time I started to make a little more money, I was introduced to the pay-per-class boutique fitness scene, and it was a dream come true for me. No longer did I have to choose between being social—going out for burgers and beers—and being healthy. There was a world where groups of us booked classes as friends and then went out for a sweaty dinner. It became my personal mecca.

So, I was dedicated, for many reasons, to the boutique scene. But despite my deep love for how these workouts fit so perfectly into my life and helped keep me sane, what I was physically doing to my body clearly wasn't good. That became apparent with the growing pain in my lower back.

As it was hurting more and more, doctors told me I needed to find a low-impact workout moving forward—no more aggressive spinning, dance classes, bootcamps, or running. That was a big blow to my daily schedule. Fitness was a huge part of my life, my identity, and in some ways, was the barrier between the old, chubby Helaine and the new, confident one who could do anything.

Boutique fitness had become a major part of my social life, too. I booked classes with my friends, took clients for work, and brought new people to see the sweat-drenched light. It was also a mental escape. Suddenly, with my back injury, I found myself sidelined from everything that made me feel good.

I'd spent years developing what I thought was a healthy regimen, falling in love with fitness, eating healthy, and embracing an active lifestyle. How on earth could I be sustaining the biggest physical setback of my life? I truly believed that I was doing it right, checking all the boxes, putting myself at the forefront of health. I should be in ninja-like shape, ready to run a Spartan race at the drop of a hat, not wearing a back brace and being told I had to be mindful of my every move.

There was also a deep fear that by removing movement in my life, I would lose all the progress I'd made in my weight loss journey and that I'd gain it all back. I didn't want to revert to who I was, because I was really starting to hit my stride, come into my own, and actually like myself.

After some time stewing over my physical pain, I started to work with a personal trainer, and really began questioning things.

Why was I injured when I thought I was doing right by my body? Is there a better way? Can I help others avoid this? What does a "low-impact" workout mean?

During one of our sessions, my trainer told me, "You know, you should try rowing. It works 85 percent of the body's muscles, burns tons of calories, and is the low-impact thing you need."

I initially wrote it off. I had no interest or experience in rowing, I thought it was for Ivy League Winklevoss-like people or CrossFit dudes. Not me and my cute SoulCycle posse.

One day I was sitting at home, depressed and full of FOMO knowing my group of friends were all taking a workout class at that moment without me, and I got a little curious about rowing. I knew nothing about it and apparently it was good for me, so I decided to do a little Googling.

As predicted, all rowers seemed to be guys doing CrossFit or Winklevoss twin clones on the water; no one looked like me or my crew. Strike 1. There were no boutique fitness classes for rowing. Strike 2. I kept picturing the ugly metal rower my grandpa kept in his basement and inadvertently wrinkled my nose in disgust thinking about that old, dusty machine. Strike 3.

But what kept me in the Google rabbit hole was learning just how good rowing was for you—it was everything anyone wanted. The nerdier the article was, the deeper the science went into why this thing was so good for you. Cardio, strength, total body, low impact: basically, the unsung hero of the gym. But who knew that? Rowing had no reputation and no fan club, but I had a strong gut feeling that it had potential.

At that moment, I started ideating on creating a new kind of workout centered around the rower—this unsung hero of the gym—that I was keen to give that makeover to. A workout experience that was fun, high energy, and torched calories; in other words, everything that drew me to the boutique fitness classes I loved, but with another key layer: really good for me and my body, able to keep me safe, and something I could do for life.

After weeks of trying to talk myself out of it, and encouraging friends to talk me out of it when I'd share the concept, there were just not enough reasons to back away. I decided the rower *was* going to get a makeover, and I was going to be the one to do it. Anyone who's built a company in any capacity knows that the right idea can quickly become an obsession. I couldn't let it go and when the thoughts couldn't escape me and I had to run out of the shower to write down new ideas while dripping water all over the floor, I knew I had to do something about it.

In the summer of 2012, I marched into dinner at Eli's on the Upper East Side for dinner with my parents and declared I was going to start a new kind of gym. Putting aside the shock (yet complete support) my parents showed me that night, uttering that sentence was the official start of my side hustle, building what became CITYROW while working a full-time job at another start-up. I had no idea what I was in for, but I had jumped in, so for me, there was no turning back.

❦

Nine intense months later, in March 2013, I was getting off the subway, about to walk into work at Olapic in our shitty shared office space in Chinatown when I looked down at an alert from Twitter on my phone. My heart stopped.

Well & Good—then the authority and voice on all things fitness with a massive profile and following—had tagged us (us being ROW NYC, the original name of CITYROW) in a tweet to their millions of followers. It was official: we were one of the hottest new fitness companies out there ("COMING SOON! We can't wait for this one!" they'd exclaimed, but never mind that we weren't even remotely close to opening). I was suddenly both excited and terrified. *Holyfuckholyfuckholyfuck*, I said to myself as I walked warily into the office, afraid that everyone in there had seen it and now knew I had a side hustle.

On the one hand, I was elated. Pure joy and excitement that this little seed idea of a company I had nurtured was starting to see its first moments *in the press*. On the other hand, I felt deep fear—not about how the hell I was going to build a successful company and all the risks I would take and the challenges I would face (those fears would come later), but more about thinking, *Holy shit, Olapic is certainly going to find out. What are they going to think? My life is over!*

Also, as the first woman at Olapic, within the male-dominated world of tech, I felt a particular responsibility to do the right thing, take care of the company, and do right by my bosses, colleagues, and team. I didn't want to let everyone down. I didn't want them to think less of me. I'd given a lot to that job, that company, and those people, and the thought that they'd be disappointed in me was too much to handle.

~◈~

As I embarked on those early days of the side hustle, I said to myself daily, *I don't know anything about business, let alone how to start a fucking company!* But a piece of advice a mentor once gave me was, "Just keep making one decision at a time to move the company forward," a phrase that guided me in those early days, and still does to this day. That, coupled with my belief in myself, propelled me forward, one small decision at a time. That's the foundation of being an entrepreneur—none of us is an oracle; we have no idea what's really going to work. We just have our own hard work and baby steps to take toward progress. There's no other way.

I also needed some help because part of the fundamental vulnerability in being an entrepreneur is having to, and being able to, ask for help. While I had the idea for CITYROW, I wasn't at all trained in fitness and knew I needed a team to help bring it to life. Asking for help has always been hard for me. I don't want people to be put off, I don't want them to think I'm needy. These are themes from middle school and being a shy kid wanting to fade into the shadows and to never be a nuisance.

Somewhere along the way, I'd trained myself to think that asking for something from someone was needy, off-putting. The minute that flipped for me was when I realized 1) people could say no, and 2) most people WANT to be helpful. I leaned in hard from there and have never been afraid to ask for help again, no matter how big or small.

What I did exceptionally well in the beginning was that I found the right people to complement me and my skills and passion. Sometimes they take the form of a guy in a blazer, sometimes they're a feisty 5'1" redhead with whom you studied abroad in college, and sometimes, they're your best friend from your last tech company who became the person you booked all your workouts with and couldn't stop talking about the idea to. That last person was Ashley Keith—she and I had met at Buddy Media and were part of that crew that got really into the boutique fitness scene together, and then went out for sweaty dinners together after taking our favorite classes. She became one of my closest friends and travel buddies, but more so, my favorite person to talk to about CITYROW. She shared the passion and always had ideas to immediately make it better. As the business started to take form, there was no way she couldn't come on board and build it alongside me, and eventually she did.

But before that, to even get to day one, I knew I needed a fitness professional to join me. I wanted to be taking the class, certainly not teaching it; I had the high-level ideas for the concept but needed someone to refine the class format and train others. I searched for months, DM'ing random people I saw who had once taught a partial rowing class or had worked at Orangetheory Fitness. I met with random people for coffee all over the city, brought a handful of potentials to a rowing certification course, flew in a trainer from Dallas...and I still could not find anyone right. The problem was that I was searching for people with experience in rowing, and it was such a new modality that the pool was small. On top of that, this was a brand new concept and a brand new company, that's a huge risk for someone to take and so when I maybe found some-one who wanted to learn more, when they found out this was a brand new idea and didn't even have a location yet, the conversa-tions died. But a trainer was not a nice-to-have, it was *the* crucial element and as I seemed to exhaust all outlets, I almost gave up.

Then, I saw Annie Mulgrew trending on the now defunct "Rate Your Burn" website as one of the best fitness instructors in Manhattan, and I recognized her immediately. We had studied abroad together in college (and almost got kidnapped in Morocco together, but that's a story for another day). Everywhere around Europe we went together, Annie would find a place for a crow pose or for a set of squats—she was all about fitness, whereas I was in the early days of my wellness journey and still focused on ensuring we were partying as hard in Europe as we were in Ann Arbor (she was also along for the party ride). Annie was an absolute blast of a person and I knew I was always in good hands—and in for a good time—with her. She was it, now I just had to convince her to do this with me.

> *Hi Friend!*
>
> *Figured I'd switch to email since that's much more civilized than FB Messenger!*
>
> *I love everything you're doing in the yoga/fitness space (everything I see on FB) and want to hear more!*
>
> *I'm actually opening a group fitness studio, which I'd love to tell you about and really just would love to catch up!*
>
> *Let me know what your schedule is like these days and hopefully we can find a time to meet for a juice/ coffee/drink!*
>
> *XO*
> *Helaine*

I DM'd her on Facebook, finally receiving a note back weeks later, then emailed her asking to have a coffee, and we finally re-connected at the Butcher's Daughter on NYC's Lower East Side over green juices. I told her all about this idea I had and she was beyond supportive. She asked to help, and offered to bring all her friends to the opening.

"Nooooooo," I said. "Thank you but actually will you be the one to develop and *teach* the class?" It didn't take much convincing—Annie bet on me just as much as I bet on her. With a foundation of trust and admiration built through traveling and adventures that junior year abroad gave us, plus a few green juices, she became the first employee and the founding instructor of CITYROW—*before ever having rowed a day in her life*. At many points in starting a company, you need complementary skill sets to take you to the next level, and Annie was the first of many of those that swooped in to make their mark.

Right before *Well & Good*'s tweet, we (by way of me asking for help from my favorite designer and developer from my old tech company) had built a basic website to assess demand for the boutique rowing concept and capture email addresses. Dan, a friend and mentor and always my first phone call in start-up business, was the first person I told about the CITYROW idea. We talked about it in a small breakout room at Olapic's shared office space, where he'd come to meet with the founders and I stole an extra thirty minutes from him to discuss it. He was a serial entrepreneur, had sold his last company to Buddy Media, and somehow became my boss in the process, one of the best I've ever had. He was even-tempered, sharp as a tack, and was constantly advocating for me, even more so than I might have advocated for myself. He'd originally placed me at Olapic and his belief in what I was building was everything to me.

He suggested doing a pop-up to assess demand, but we found a better way to do that more efficiently with a "Sign up here to be the first to know" section of the new CITYROW website. The goal was to get three hundred email addresses. If we could pull that off, then we'd pull the trigger to figure out moving forward and opening a rowing studio. After the *Well & Good* tweet, other outlets, including the *New York Times*, the *New York Post*, and the *New York Daily News*, picked up on our concept and soon we had over 1,500 signups to be the first to know about "the hottest new thing in group fitness"—all WELL before we had a space, opened our doors, or even had an inkling on *how* to open our doors.

I cannot emphasize enough how huge and encouraging it was.

Crap, I also said to myself at the time. *Now I actually have to figure out how to do this thing we said we were going to do.*

Any big move in a company—bringing on a new hire, pitching an investor, working with a vendor, not to mention starting it in the first place—involves being vulnerable. It is like dating, when you think or say, *This is all of me. Do you like me? Do you accept me? Should we keep this thing up?* As a founder, the business is an extension of me, making that vulnerability extend beyond business and into the personal. As Brené Brown says, once you step into the arena, be prepared to be pummeled.

To that end, spring into summer of 2013 was just a grind. I was spending sixty hours a week at Olapic and whatever was left over I scraped from the bottom of the energy barrel to focus on CITYROW. I talked to people, got advice, made connections, and spent a few thousand dollars from my personal paychecks here and there. Eventually, the start-up lawyer who'd been helping me was ready to file our articles of incorporation and the trademark application to go along with it. This legal work was the first real bill the company received and I realized we needed a company bank account. After opening a business account at Citibank, I switched to my personal Citibank profile and looked long and hard at the savings account I'd worked really hard to build up. I took a deep breath, and hit "transfer" to the new business bank account. My fledgling company had its first $25,000.

Now it was time to think about where to get the rest of the start-up capital we'd need. I knew very little about fundraising, and the only experience/example I had with anyone raising money was with my boss and friends in the tech start-up world. This was a whole new language for me, based on ideas like "valuations," "notes," "discounts," and "cap tables." Luckily, I'm a quick study and had the right people around to guide me. Almost right away I learned that in the early days of fundraising, for investors it's about betting on an idea, and the valuation (i.e., how much the company is projected to be worth) is as simple as what they're willing to pay. There's no clear path or one way to do things, so I just went with a number, and it stuck.

Given my previous, and only, exposure to fundraising, I decided to raise money like any good tech company (although technically we were a brick-and-mortar business, I was a techie at heart and knew no other way at the time). I chose a clean million dollars for our valuation and got to raising money around that, even though I had very little idea of how much I would actually need to start and run a business.

It was terrifying to ask my parents, my grandma, my uncle Steven, even some close friends to invest, and I made all the classic mistakes of fundraising. I had the mentality that they were supporting me (versus a viable business concept) and worried incessantly about losing their money. Instead, I should've thought of my first raise as an incredible opportunity for my loved ones to get in early and make a ton of money down the line. This was eight-year-old insecure Helaine getting the best of me, not badass Helaine who would have interviewed every potential investor to ask them how they'd add value and make them realize what an amazing opportunity they were getting into at the ground level. If they weren't behind it, they'd get cut.

Shooting from the hip, I figured $150,000 was enough to get us up and running: $50,000 for the studio buildout, $50,000 for things like equipment, and $50,000 for things like legal work and anything else business-related.

Spoiler alert: $150,000 was not enough. Not anywhere close.

I learned almost any company needs more start-up capital and runway than you originally think. Period. Luckily, I also learned that *when someone (good) wants to give you money, you take it.* Don't think, just take it. So, when I was introduced to another $100,000 investor through a connection from Olapic, I didn't think twice, I took it.

Once the company had a few dollars to its name, it was time to start investing it in our build, but to do so, I needed some physical checks. So much banking and finance is done now via digital or electronic modes, but in July 2013, the only thing that meant being legit was the big book of checks. They came in an oversized binder and perforated pages. Opening it meant business, literally and figuratively.

On my Olapic lunch hour, I snuck over to the nearest Citibank branch. I loathe dealing with institutions and paperwork so the process of getting the bank account set up and the checks ordered was a big mental drain for me. Luckily, those big-ass checks were a great reward for dealing with that bureaucracy. And for the first time, our company's name would be printed on a piece of paper I held.

That same week, my attorney Jared was preparing to file a trademark for our company, which was still at the time called ROW NYC.

Right after I picked up my prized big checkbook and left the bank, weirdly excited to open it up later and make a few key payments that were pending, Jared called.

"Helaine, I have some bad news," he said.

"Oh no," I replied, immediately spiraling into thinking there was no way we could open a rowing studio, that it was all over before I'd even used my big checkbook. "What is it?"

"There's a non-profit organization called Row New York that's been around for quite a while, and they aren't thrilled with our use of the name ROW NYC," he explained, then dropped the real bomb: "Well, that's an understatement. We *can't* use that name for the company. I'm really sorry, but you've got to go back to the drawing board."

I stopped in my tracks and immediately burst into tears on Eldridge Street right in front of my favorite dumpling spot (Vanessa's), with thousands of people brushing by me, and the smell of garbage and rotten fish wafting into my nose.

"But I just got the *checks*," I wailed between tears. "*Now* what do I do?"

I was already comfortable with the ROW NYC name, we had been written about in the press under that name, and we had the big checks! In my mind, it might as well have been tattooed on my forehead.

My friends really helped me through that first big tidal wave; in particular, Ashley stepped in to save the day. She's always been the temperature gauge and visionary for everything creative we've done as a company, so she took the reins and set up a brainstorm for ideas for our new name.

"Okay, everyone. When you have a moment, please take a look at this Word doc and add in your new name ideas," she said to a group of us who'd gathered at her impeccably decorated sunken living room of her apartment on the Upper East Side to help "Namestorm." "Nothing is too out there—let's think outside the box!"

This was the first time I'd really needed my crew behind me, and boy did they show up. While I hadn't always had this support system of friends, when I did find them (my early friends from Encampment youth group, the fifty kids from my teen tour that traveled in from all over the country and showed up at my sixteenth birthday party, my high school friends from the softball team welcoming me into their long-established crew), they were rock solid and stayed that way through my life. The hodgepodge of friends and colleagues and acquaintances who informed and helped me with the early CITYROW concept was no different— they were my brain trust, and the support was real, recognized, and appreciated. By the end of that first session, we had pages and pages of potential names and while I was still rattled and upset that we had to make this pivot in the first place, we had a path over the first big hump.

I stop short of saying that everything happens for a reason, because that saying is overdone, and kind of bullshit. However, that day the real CITYROW was born, and paved the way for us to scale nationwide outside of NYC in a way that the previous name could never allow.

～

Meanwhile, the search for the space was well underway. And at the *very* same time I started looking for real estate for CITYROW, the Olapic founders asked me to help them find new office space, too. What were the chances I'd become a real estate expert for not one, but two companies?

One summer morning before work, my broker Elliot and I met with a building manager named Zeke, who showed us the fourth floor of a commercial building on West 26th Street for CITYROW. Then, in the most surreal of twists, that afternoon I was touring with the Olapic founders and their broker and we ended up visiting *that very same building* that *very same day* to look at a new office space for us on the sixth floor. By some miracle, Zeke didn't blow my cover, or even act like he knew me. He must've been saying to himself, "What in the actual fuck is this girl looking for, a gym or a tech start-up?"

It's no wonder, then, that my back issues that started in 2012 got *really* bad throughout 2013. I think in addition to the stress of juggling two full-time jobs, I had a lot of guilt compounding for spending so much time on my side hustle. Even though I was still over-performing at my job at Olapic, I felt like I was betraying them in some way, that I wasn't giving 100 percent to them, despite still doing an exceptional job. I didn't worry so much about letting anyone down on the CITYROW side, at least not yet. I was the founder and could disappoint myself all day long.

What I've learned since then is that the notion of giving 100 percent is ridiculous because not all tanks are the same size or need the same amount of power. It's more about having enough for your personal output. And for many jobs these days, there's no limit to what you can give to it. I was certainly doing more than enough to support my job at Olapic (and got beautiful performance reviews regularly to prove it). I just knew I had more to dedicate some-where, and it wasn't going into my day job, because I was putting it into a personal passion. The Helaine of today wouldn't feel guilty because I know a balanced life is paramount. But for me at that moment in time, the guilt was all-consuming.

As someone who always wants to do my best at everything I set my mind to, knowing that all my energies weren't going to my day job weighed on me, and that made my back feel so much worse. I hadn't learned yet the lesson that you can manage your time but it takes a more sophisticated person to manage your energy. It's all part of self-awareness and knowing both what drains you and what fills you up.

Even in the middle of the craziness of a start-up launch, you have to pay attention to yourself. For example, take a

temperature gauge during the day and see how you feel doing different things and then establish some boundaries (which I'll talk about in more detail in another chapter). It's the only way to head off burnout.

If only I had known then what I know now.

As Labor Day approached, I had been looking for space in earnest for months, finding spaces that looked great only for them to fall through during the LOI (letter of intent) phase once they learned that we were 1) a gym and 2) this was a first location for a new concept—apparently that was risky.

I was starting to get defeated.

One day my brother called me—he'd been looking at space for me between work and said he'd found something within budget right in the heart of USQ with a lot of potential. I met him there after work and it was a video editing studio on the 15th floor of an office building. It had some break out offices but if you took the walls down, it could be beautiful. It had these old big almost bay windows that looked out over 5th avenue and with high ceilings, the light flowed through. It would have its challenges but it was worth a shot.

The other reason this building could work was because it was owned by a single family—not a huge real estate development group. The building manager was a lawyer who worked out of the building and he was eager to rent the space. He was pushing me to move quickly and the Thursday before labor day he sent me the contract and said—have this signed by Tuesday or we're going with someone else.

He could smell my desperation and was using it against me.

That weekend I had a wedding but was distracted by the looming lease. I had no money for big, fancy real estate lawyers but convinced my dad (a residential real estate attorney) and a random person I met at the wedding (a litigator) to review the lease at a high level with me. My dad was far from thrilled with this ask—apparently these types of real estate law are quite different—but he took a spin through and between the two of them, I didn't sign, but I had notes back to him Tuesday morning.

That afternoon, still recovering from the wedding, Ashley and I went for a walk along the east river uptown. We were constantly brainstorming at this point and that night I remember telling her, "if this space doesn't work out, I don't know if I can keep going".

I was hitting a first breaking point and as excited as I was to see this through, the constantly loss after loss on real estate was wearing me down. Not to mention doing two jobs and holding the guilt from doing both!

Luckily, after some finagling and wheeling and dealing that following week, we got to terms and there was just one thing left to do as we signed the lease—sign a personal "Good Guy Guarantee". I learned this was a special NYC clause to prevent squatters in spaces wherein if a company had to fold, the person who signed the lease would be on the hook for the rent personally until the keys were given back to the Landlord so they could re-rent it. Despite my dad not being thrilled once again (I was a pretty good kid but boy was I testing my parents in my mid-20's!) he said he wouldn't stop me from signing it.

Unfortunately, the landlord said that I didn't have enough net worth to be a viable signee so someone would have to co-sign it with me. My parents were out, no way my dad was going to go for that and wouldn't encourage my grandma to either (turns out having a lawyer in the family is a good and bad thing at times).

This exhausted my family so it was time to go to friends and early investors. It was a big ask for someone to go-guarantee the lease with me and it was hard to approach people. It was one thing to ask for money but another entirely to ask them to do a huge favor for the company. I was willing to compensate people and eventually, one of my old bosses and her husband expressed interest in learning more.

We started chatting daily and I immediately said, "Thank you, this is a huge unlock for the business and I'd be happy to give you additional equity in the business". At this point I'd learned that advisors typically see a fractional % of shares and founding employees can see anywhere from 1-10 percent (There are massive exceptions to all of these)—so I'd figured we'd land in the 2-3 percent range. When they finally got back to me—they suggested an astounding 10 percent. I was shocked. I was sitting at my parents' house, borrowing my mom's office, and sneaking in an email check during a Jewish holiday gathering. I sat in my mom's oversized office chair with my dress, stockings and pumps on the verge of tears. We were far apart on what we were each thinking. This was going to be a challenge.

Over the next week we exchanged emails and calls—I shared my thinking and rationale behind 3 percent they dug in at 10 percent. I flexed up to 5 percent, they dug their heels in further. I went up to 6.5 percent. They did not move. They knew I needed this to move forward and they had me in a bind. They knew too much—that if they didn't sign it we wouldn't get this lease so they were holding it above my head.

There was nothing I could do. Every day I would get pressure from the landlord to sign the lease and he would threaten to pull the deal. I placated him with the fact that we were finalizing and should have it soon—I broke down in tears nightly as the pressure mounted.

It was the night before the drop dead closing—I had just left dinner with my brother in Brooklyn and needed to have one more 8pm call with my old boss and her husband to try and get them to see that 10 percent was ludicrous.

They were not going to budge, it was 10 percent or no deal.

I was infuriated—I felt taken advantage of, wronged and angry. But there was nothing I could do.

I remembered the advice I'd gotten, you just need to keep making one decision at a time to keep the company moving forward, there was only one way forward and I begrudgingly decided to take it.

From there, things moved very quickly. Less than two months later, in November 2013, we were gearing up for a January launch. It felt like the whole world—or at least the entire fitness community— was waiting for us expectantly.

Meanwhile, balancing two start-ups, my own and someone else's, continued to get to me and I was working myself to the ground. I was dodging Olapic work trips to Argentina to meet our tech team, doing morning physical therapy or breakfast meetings daily, working hard at Olapic, working on the CITYROW financial model I was pulling out of my ass at lunchtime, then either doing a six-thirty or seven-thirty SoulCycle evening class, on a day when I thought my back was okay enough to make it through, or doing more CITYROW work after my first workday was done, then falling dead asleep to the world. If I made it to dinner with friends during that time, they could practically see the waves of stress steaming off me.

Later that November, I had to go to LA for a work trip exactly when the rowers—the centerpiece of our CITYROW business—were getting delivered. I couldn't be there. The guilt and the feeling that I was disappointing people, which was already everywhere, started to pile up, this time on the CITYROW side. Plus, this was a moment I wanted to be there for (and be able to take photos of for Instagram!).

We were weeks away from opening and learning on the fly. *Do we need a cash register? How do you work a POS system? OMG, we need T-shirts. How do we send emails? Do we need staff?* Everything was a fire drill.

I had wanted to resign from Olapic before and should have, but I was afraid to let the stability go, and I really needed that end-of-year bonus. So instead, I was burning both ends of the candle right down to the wick and burning myself out in the process.

But when you're that passionate about something, with deep conviction and drive to make it happen, you push yourself further, and then some. It was late nights and early mornings (and I'm not really a night owl OR a morning person!), and it taxed me, physically and emotionally.

I was pure adrenaline and cortisol (and might still be). I somehow dug even deeper in the weeks leading up to launch. In the beginning, while everyone pitched in and helped, it was a lot...and I had reached a point where I literally couldn't walk.

"You look like death," Ashley commented, not unkindly.

It was six forty-five at night and Ashley had stopped by on opening day that January, missing the six-thirty class by a good ten minutes but still eager to check in and see how day one went, generously helping me wipe down some sweaty mats after class was over. I had started our grand opening day at five o'clock in the morning, opening the doors for our six o'clock class, then went to work, then came back to CITYROW during lunch, and then again after work. Also that day, after seeing the cash register ding for the first time, I resigned from Olapic, giving them one month's notice.

~

I woke up from surgery pain-free for the first time in two years. I spent those next forty-eight hours strolling around the halls with my walker or responding to tweets about CITYROW from my hospital bed, all while on a boatload of pain meds.

Meanwhile, I was immensely grateful—our small but growing crew was at the studio taking care of business, and I made my big return two weeks after my surgery because I had a TV interview scheduled with *New York One.*

In the early days, I used to fear that this may not work out. In fact, data articulating the likely success of a start-up shows it's more likely that it won't work out. That's a terrifying thought right as you're about to pour yourself into something that's far from a certain outcome... highlighting how intense it is to really put yourself out there.

But underneath the deep vulnerability I was experiencing I knew that no matter what, I would negotiate our surroundings, that I would somehow figure it out, and that there was no one else I'd want to bet on than me. In the back of my mind, I also knew that, in the worst-case scenario if that first rowing studio didn't pan out, we'd pivot to a co-working space, yoga studio, or moonlight with Bar Mitzvah parties.

I didn't end up taking my first CITYROW class until November 2014, ten months after we opened. In all the days leading up to it, I felt like such an imposter; here I am, founder of a fitness concept, but I've never felt weaker and haven't even taken the class. Unfortunately, the notion of "imposter syndrome"—which is problematic but something a lot of people, especially women, experience—will show up again in my story. But in the early days of CITYROW and especially during my back crisis, it was a throwback to my childhood. Many have walked in those same shoes in their own story, but for me, the particular experience of being an overweight kid and teen added another layer of complexity to deciding to be a fitness mogul. Starting a company is hard regardless of who you are, but the industry I chose (or that chose me) brings in my personal identity and a layer of personal vulnerability beyond the professional that makes things even more complex. So, I may always struggle at times with being a founder, and a highly visible one at that, in the fitness industry, but the truth is that there's no way to start a company without being vulnerable in pretty much every single way.

CHAPTER 5

DEEP WATER

At this point, I was running on coffee, adrenaline, and the excitement of getting something off the ground, this little thing we called CITYROW.

The reality of running CITYROW, however, was that it was actually a massive undertaking. It felt like we were in over our heads. Instead of all the excitement and possibility of what it could be, which kept me going throughout the uncertainty and the side hustle pre-launch, now I was faced with actually operating it—the first "finish line" was just the beginning. This included the people I needed on my team, which makes or breaks a business (I knew how to hire and manage account managers, not hourly workers, instructors, and consultants, which was the new job at hand), and the hours I suddenly had to work. Hello, nights and weekends!

The operations alone were a constant set of tidal waves, and that was before scratching the surface on what would be the most challenging part: fundraising.

~

Money, capital, was—and *is*—always critical. What preoccupied me in those early days was how we would be able to cover our ongoing costs, like rent and operating expenses. From there, the goal was building revenue, and, pretty importantly (vitally important actually), could I pay myself? Could I pay anyone else? Could we use revenue to grow, that is, eventually open another location?

While I had a little commission cash saved away from my last job, which bootstrapped the company pre-opening, I couldn't cover it all and the studio wouldn't build and grow itself. I would need to raise additional capital from other people.

At my Buddy Media job, all my colleagues and bosses were betting on me to make deals, and I succeeded. But now, I was ready to let go of my safety net and the security of someone else paying me regularly, and bet on myself. This was a big step both tactically and personally—I finally had the confidence to choose me, *invest* in me over anyone else. I had gained that confidence working out there in the corporate/established start-up world and it was time to put it to the test. I was all nerves and a dash of excitement.

Fundraising was the best (or worst) possible first test. My first thought was: This was going to be easy, right? The market was frothy and start-ups were getting funded left and right. I'd been a part of two successful ones already and it seemed like I was good at this business/people/sales thing. Despite a lot of cards stacked against me (being a female and start-up life in general), I was ready to have faith, and as I'd said, and came to really believe, bet on myself above all else. I assumed other people would be lining up to do the same.

And at first, they were. Even though I was terrified at times, I did it—I raised $250,000 in a "Friends and Family" round (often the first stage of investment for young companies). After I put that very first check in myself, my friend and mentor Dan (the same sage and advisor whom I introduced to you earlier) put in the next check, followed by my parents, then my grandma, then my uncle, then almost all my former bosses, and finally some friends of friends who'd been hearing about what we were doing.

But the tactics of taking capital were new to me. I'd read about it time and time again but had zero experience in the legal and finance side of what went on behind the scenes. Luckily, I had some good people to show me the way. We started from scratch.

"A company's valuation," Dan told me, "is simply what someone is willing to pay to invest in it. So just get it done."

"Sure, got it," I said. *But also, how*?! I wondered.

There is no traditional school for the experience of entrepreneurship. Yes, there are videos and books and online masterclasses, but *so* much is learned by doing, asking, seeking, and making the call (and making mistakes, lots of them).

On day one, I knew nothing about fundraising and valuations and all the nuances of money in business, so I did what I do best. I got creative, asked for help, and made an educated guess, landing on $1 million as the valuation of CITYROW for that first round of fundraising. It seemed to make sense to me—it was a nice round number and it felt big enough, but not so huge as to be overwhelming. Also, it fit within the standard tech fundraising framework (something I'd learned from all the pre-opening business reading I'd been doing) of giving away 15 to 25 percent of the company (in equity) at every round. So, if our total capital raised goal was $200,000 to $250,000, that math worked in the most basic sense. In retrospect, that $1 million I landed on was too low—$2 million to $4 million would have made more sense and would have been doable given the times and traction in the market.

"Thank you *so* much," I'd say in the early days, practically crying with gratitude to anyone who handed me a check or wired money into the CITYROW account. "I'll work as hard as I possibly can and make you so proud. We will succeed."

I had this dynamic all wrong and it took me years to get it right in my head. Investors should (and eventually would) thank me for letting them be part of this company, letting them have equity and be a witness to and partner in my hard work and hustle for the value-creation and growth. But that's a hard switch to flip and especially hard for people like me with any kind of insecurities (and for women in general, but we'll get into that later).

After that initial Friends and Family round, we opened our doors in earnest and we had enough cash coming in to cover costs. Even paying myself $40,000 a year as a salary (let this be another example that starting a company is not as glamorous as some people make it out to be. It almost always involves some sacrifices, if not downright poverty for a while) and making some light improvements in the business, we were cash flow-positive on this tiny studio in NYC. That was something to celebrate.

❧

Why did people invest in CITYROW? They mostly bet on the jockey. And while I might be 5'10", that jockey was me.

Mike was a wealthy contractor I met through a friend at Olapic, and after meeting him and showing him our raw, soon-to-be CITYROW studio space in Union Square in NYC, he said to me bluntly, "I'm not sure about this rowing thing, but I'm all in on the Helaine train."

Mike would go on to being not only a supporter, but mentor, confidant, and partner in many areas as I developed as a CEO. His early support made him one of the most critical members of the CITYROW crew for its tenure.

Another early CITYROW investor was one of my favorite people from Buddy Media, Pam, a woman who managed accounts like a queen, upsold, and threw us project managers commission opportunities every time she could. I told her what I was doing and she wanted in.

It was really hard for me to ask her for the actual money (back to that insecurity dynamic), but she didn't blink and on the spot wrote me a check for $10,000.

Shortly thereafter, Pam, my friend Ashley (whom I worked with at Buddy Media, became best friends, and who later became my CITYROW co-founder), and I were celebrating over a wine-soaked dinner.

"Pam," I said. "Remember that the grand opening is next week. You need to be there!"

"Oh, I wouldn't miss it," she replied. "Should I bring my bathing suit?"

I laughed, thinking she was joking. Ashley—ever my complementary counterpart—looked deeply puzzled.

"Why would you bring a bathing suit?" Ashley asked.

Pam suddenly looked a little embarrassed, not something I was used to seeing from her.

"Isn't CITYROW a bunch of small pools we row in?"

We set her straight and the three of us laughed for about an hour. I now think of this story, especially in my down moments, as an important reminder that so many people really were willing to bet on me—"hitch on to the Helaine train" like my contractor/investor Mike said—even without having any idea what I was trying to build. I tapped into that feeling when I needed to get myself through the lows that came later.

But those were the early days with friends and family. They knew me, they'd watched me, they'd seen me in action, and just like me, they were eager to see where this train could go, with the right amount of fuel and pointed in the right direction. Every single one of my former bosses was involved in that first round of funding, which was both a major confidence boost and a reality check. Not only was I putting my own money where my mouth was, but lots of other people were too.

❧

The day we opened, we were profitable on a cash basis. Just saying those words out loud still shocks me. We'd worked hard to get a critical mass of interested people in the CITYROW concept, so when we opened our doors to sell class packs, people legitimately rushed in. We didn't spend a dime on marketing, we'd just hit the market at the right time, built enough buzz, and the demand was there.

Now that the obstacle of money was out of the way, at least for a few minutes, I settled into running CITYROW day to day. A brick-and-mortar business is a fucking beast; it was non-stop, we were open from five o'clock in the morning until nine o'clock at night. Almost immediately, we faced a never-ending barrage of absurd problems like our HVAC system breaking (imagine having no air-conditioning, much less air flow, in a room full of sweaty people rowing their asses off), people not showing up for classes they'd signed up for and not wanting to pay when that happened, and realizing we needed an entirely new gym floor. It was like learning a new language; I had never even heard these words before and was constantly frustrated with what I didn't know. If I never hear the term "HVAC" again, it'll be too soon.

I realized soon after opening that we might need to hire people. Obviously, right? Not to me at first. It truly never occurred to me that we would need, for example, someone to work the front desk and check people in and engage with customers. With my naive energy, I just figured the instructors would be able to do it before teaching their classes—problem solved!

But the business was busy around the clock, including nights and weekends; it was not my familiar nine to five (ish) work. Even with me practically sleeping in the studio (forget dinner with friends) and mostly joyfully soaking up every second of this new venture, I needed some serious help, not least because at that point (for the first two months of CITYROW's operations), I was still working my full-time job at the tech company.

I'm not a morning person, especially on Saturdays, so I immediately begged a couple of my friends to work the front desk at that time, and they readily agreed. I'll never forget everyone who stepped up to help, especially in those early days. From building rowers and installing speakers, to setting up cubbies and filling spots when we wanted to stack the class for a VIP, my people showed up. But it was another thing to require them to work certain shifts.

I arrived at the studio one day, mid-shift, and noted their open bottle of champagne, and the two half-full glasses they were sipping from as they laughed with some customers coming in. I laughed too. They were helping me out and having fun while they were at it so how could I complain? The next week I had a bottle waiting for them when they got there. The "work hard, play hard" concept never rang truer.

I had to get up to warp speed, learning about managing people faster than I'd ever had before—how to pay them, how to interview them, how to find reliable ones (which, by the way, weren't always the people you thought) to work a regular weekly set of shifts for hourly pay, and how to manage the distribution of studio door keys, especially when your lead instructor loses hers every four days. That's before anyone has any scheduling conflicts or issues with clients. Yes, I was in deep (over my head) but I was also loving the thrill of this new, unchartered waters, learning the ropes, and figuring out how to stay afloat.

Then there was the lawsuit we were pounded with in our first four days of opening. Have I mentioned yet that starting a business is trial by fire? Well, it is.

The issue was that we shared an air conditioning duct with the publishing company next door, which did not appreciate the sounds of constant booming music and screaming instructors emanating from our space with zero soundproofing. So, they reached out to the building manager and served us with an injunction to close down CITYROW.

It was really overwhelming and stressful. It felt like the end was here before we even got our legs.

In retrospect, opening a fitness studio on the fifteenth floor of an otherwise corporate building might not have been the best call, but even though the landlord was shady (and my gut told me it wasn't the best spot for us), no one else would rent a space to us without a business track record, so I had no choice at the time. Lesson learned: If it seems too good to be true, it probably is.

I called up my attorney, Jared, who, less than twelve months before, had explained to me what an operating agreement was and helped me incorporate the first CITYROW entity. Now he had to go fight for us.

We went back and forth on how to handle this for a while and Jared was confident we'd find a solution. I was a ball of anxiety. On the day of the judgment, Jared said he'd stop by the studio after, regardless of what happened in court. That day he jogged up the fifteen flights of stairs (the elevator was broken, a recurring nightmare over the years for us), opened the door to the studio, saw me, and with a broad grin, unbuttoned the top few buttons of his dress shirt to reveal a CITYROW T-shirt underneath.

"We're good. We can continue to operate!" he crowed. My own personal superhero.

As a result of his ninja-like legal maneuverings, we ended up having to put in a limiter on our noise and volume, and agree to a change of flooring (both big expenses, especially in those early days), but we would stay open!

Numerous early trials aside, all signs pointed to the fact that CITYROW was working.

We had raised the seed capital, figured out how to run and operate a fitness studio, and we were profitable(!). People came to the studio. Better, they came back and paid money to do so. They bought ten-packs and twenty-packs, and wanted private instructions and buy-outs for private and corporate groups. Other brands came to us wanting something new and paid partnership opportunities flourished. Our brand was building and the community was fueled by strong word-of-mouth referrals.

It wasn't just clients; the press also fell in love with CITYROW—in a big way. Within our first six months, we were in the *New York Times, People, Harper's Bazaar, Vogue*, and many more. We were media darlings across TV, print, and digital. There were nonstop in-bound queries about CITYROW, and I was starting to get profiled—this was all without a dedicated PR person. Something was resonating, the CITYROW wave was building, and we were riding it hard.

Supermodels like Iman came in, the *Real Housewives of New York City* (who were scorching hot at the time) came in, and Hugh Jackman came in, who's a different kind of scorching hot.

Most importantly, clients got what we were going for at CITYROW: they loved the workout and they felt good (well, they felt sore, but in a good way). They said it was the best workout and community out there, and we agreed.

The goal, our why for starting CITYROW, was wanting a better way to work out, a smarter way to move your body. It was my "Why do I have a back injury when I've been working out so much and should be in the best shape of my life?" why, and it was the answer I'd been looking for, and realized many others would benefit from as well. A safe, smart way to move your body, push yourself, elevate your heart rate for cardio benefits, and lift weights, smartly and safely to build muscle, all in one. It was a dream to create this in one product that was effective, yet safe and intelligently designed. We didn't know if consumers would *feel it*. When they did, and they told us, either after class, before their next one, or just because they kept on coming, we knew we'd made magic.

There were some really beautiful moments as people talked about this rowing revolution that we were leading. That all gave me, and our young team, so much energy and confidence, not to mention validation of our business, that this thing really had legs to stand on, and to grow on.

I'll say it time and again: Trial by fire and learning by doing is the truest element of starting and running your own company. In any business, you can plan and think and create but there's nothing, and I mean nothing, like living and breathing and doing it. Despite all my preparation and anticipation and thinking ahead, there were curveballs, tidal waves, and problems I never saw coming. That's a start-up, and that's life—you can listen to the cliche "Be prepared for the unexpected," but the truth is nothing can fully prepare you. You just have to take each wave as it comes. Even better if you like surfing the monster ones—thrive on the ability to solve those problems. If not, this path might not be for you. I've never done any extreme sports, but I'm one of the crazies who courageously faces these business waves, challenge after challenge. I grew to not necessarily love them, but tolerate them and enjoy the process of getting through the small day-to-day problems and the big, monstrous ones that threatened our very existence.

The early days of CITYROW were full of anticipation of what could be. We were living a dream in the present but always knew this was bigger, way bigger. We were never planning to open one studio and then call it a day. I had then, have today, and will always have a huge vision and always think as big as possible.

So, as we started mitigating the day-to-day drama, I immediately turned to how and where do we grow. The natural next step felt like a second location. The first location was very much a test of the product, and despite many curveballs, we were passing with flying colors.

In my view then, it was time to build a flagship, a true physical representation of this powerful and growing brand with national and global media attention, the premier company we were building.

So, we hired retail brokers and started looking at spaces, and once again, reality bit me, hard. While looking for ground floor real estate to make that premier representation a reality, we were in a whole new realm of pricing—the big leagues—and didn't quite (um, at all) have the cash on hand to back it up...yet.

We eventually found a fixer-upper—and did it ever need a lot of work—but we dove in and started working out the details for the second location of CITYROW, on New York's Upper East Side.

CHAPTER 6

THE FLOOD

It would take upwards of $1 million to build out and open a second location, probably way more, a far cry from the initial $150,000 to build the first location and far more than we could cover with cash flows from the original Union Square location.

I started fundraising for this second location. On the one hand, we had a real product, a physical studio people could touch and feel to understand the brand and consider investing. But at the same time, the studio was not as fancy as the other players at the time and we had very little data on our economics to prove anything meaningful just yet. This time I went a degree further, getting referred to friends of our first batch of investors and chasing down every lead I got, raising from as many angel investors as I could find while starting to talk to venture capital funds.

This round of fundraising was a slow process once again, and we signed the lease for the second location on the Upper East Side

while I was square in the middle of the raise. It was a risky decision but we needed to sign the lease or lose it, so I made that for-
ward-moving yet scary move on the chess board, betting on me/
my ability to raise it as we opened, and hoping cash flows from the
first location would help us out. In retrospect, it was more than a
little risky but I knew it was going to work. We'd find a way and we
had to keep moving because stagnancy was death at a start-up.

On the Upper East Side, I was literally knee-deep in sawdust,
whitewall, cement, and power tools, doing daily inspections of our
new space, while at the same time my phone was pressed between
my ear and shoulder as I frantically tried to network with potential investors and get some major traction moving. It was something I was having a lot of trouble drumming up for this soon-to-be
two-location brick-and-mortar company.

This round was when I really had to start confronting the fact
that CITYROW wasn't a tech company; it was a physical gym,
so no matter how big the vision, most of my legacy contacts in
tech were relatively useless. I had to build a whole new network.
Because of that, I continued to struggle getting money in the door
in the near term when we desperately needed it.

And forget institutional investors or large funds. We were too
small for the big retail investors: "Maybe when you have ten-plus
locations," they'd say. We only had one location operating successfully at that point, and still no real track record in business. It was
a weird in-between stage: success but seeming failure in the objec-
tive to raise capital, which would allow us to grow. Rowing was also
a pretty new workout modality at that point and I spent most of our
first five years with investors convincing them that rowing was the
next big thing. If I had a dollar for everyone who told me to market
to collegiate rowers, I wouldn't have had to raise any money at all!
But that's not who we were and from experience, they weren't into

what we were offering, so I listened, nodding to make them feel heard, and plowed on.

Without a large investor to help lead this as a priced round, I kept raising via angel investors. Here's where I kept hitting the pavement hard and eventually found some success, tapping into my people, my network, my network's networks, and sales skills to hustle one angel at a time who saw and liked what we were doing. Some of them were even big CITYROW fans. Those $25,000, $50,000, and $100,000, and checks became the place I could win in those days and how I kept CITYROW afloat.

There were true angels like my friend Jeff, who sat watching me as a ball of stress over coffee one day, panicked about how we were going to pay for this new studio and frustrated there weren't more small retail funds willing to give us a shot. We had something big, but I couldn't find the key to taking it to the next level.

"Do you need money?" he asked me, point blank.

"Yes!" I almost wailed, knowing payroll was coming up in two days and we were cutting this one too close for comfort.

I sent him the documents and wire information and with a few taps on his phone, a minute later I got an alert on mine: $25,000 was available immediately, sent from Jeff.

As hammers kept swinging on our second location, I raised what I thought we'd needed from the onset, but it turned out that the buildout cost for the second location ended up being ten times the amount we spent on the first location.

We're fucked and in serious debt, I remember thinking to myself, sitting in a cold sweat. That's how I felt on the inside but I also knew I had to keep it all together on the outside, for my team, our clients, our investors. I had to be confident with a plan, but I felt like I was simultaneously unraveling.

Remember Mike, our amazing contractor/investor? We owed him $350,000 for the construction of the second Upper East Side space, and I had to go to him with the news that we couldn't pay him even in monthly installments. It was one of my toughest business conversations (and I've had so many there's no way I could even count them) with someone I considered my mentor and someone I deeply respected. I felt like I failed him.

And that, my friends, is the reality of start-ups, money, and fundraising.

Eventually, we had a come-to-Jesus call and decided to do the rest of the construction and log the money we owed Mike as a long-term loan, which made sense from a business/financial perspective but emotionally was hard. We'd paper the construction debt as money we owed him at a future date, with no huge monthly installments but also not an equity investment in the business for him. It was the best solution, but I didn't like the idea of not being able to pay our bills. This was the start of me feeling like I was digging myself a hole that I'd never be able to climb out of.

I'd love to say that things went up from there—like the entrepreneurial gods waved a magic wand and wiped away the stress and struggle of the past few months—but I would be lying.

It was a shit show from day one. No. From well before day one/opening day.

We had chosen the architect who had designed the vaunted Drybar locations, a business that was an absolute phenomenon when it opened (you mean I can go somewhere and get an affordable and amazing blowout, sip champagne, and watch romantic comedies? *I'm in.*) and its founder—Alli Webb—was one of a handful of women whom I looked up to as someone who'd pioneered retail and built a cult brand.

We were determined to bring the vision for our second CITYROW location to life in a new and exciting way, an extension of our growth. While we hired the best architect we could find, and had dreams of this being the secret bullet, what we actually needed was a visionary designer alongside a competent architect. We loved our team of architects and they did a good job, but we were left disappointed because our expectations were for our version of the yellow hair dryer motif from Drybar. As it turns out, that's not an architect, that's an epic brand designer, which we did not have or use. Another expensive and hard lesson.

Next, we found out we had asbestos in the walls, and had to tear them apart to get that abated. Delays after delays, which, of course, delayed our second location opening, and delayed that second revenue stream. The waiting has always been one of the hardest parts for me. I'm a doer, I love to execute, and when things are quiet and I'm waiting on others, I feel useless. During those months of waiting on the second location, I was chomping at the bit to grow, yet handcuffed by asbestos specialists and NYC permits.

Once we got the green light, our amazing construction team got to work, quickly. It was the fourth quarter of 2015 and if we moved fast, we could open in early January, the most popular time for the fitness world. There was no way, especially after all this delay, that we could miss a January opening. We also had a ticking time bomb on paying rent. Our landlord had agreed to three months of free rent (often given to businesses to build out a raw space without the burden of rent) but after those three months, we were on the hook for over $20,000 a month...regardless if we had revenue coming in or not.

Alongside construction, we were preparing to essentially double the business operations, double the staff, and go from operating and managing one studio to two, across the city from each other. It was extremely hectic, stressful, and wildly exciting. We were going to have a ground floor storefront in NYC! We were entering the big leagues!

By mid-December, construction was humming along. One of the key pieces of the buildout was that in the second space we needed to upgrade its ADA requirements (essentially make it accessible for all those with disabilities and have a ramp/wheelchair access) or be in violation of a law before we were up and running. We had planned to convert a back ventilation screen into a door with a ramp and cut a hole adjacent to the door to serve as the louver for the HVAC (essentially how air will circulate in/out depending on the time of year).

It wasn't a tiny hole; it was a seven-by-five-foot hole, thirty square feet in total, that I planned to cut into the side of a 170-unit condo building in the heart of Manhattan.

During the summer prior, before the final lease negotiations, part of the lease negotiating process was that we had to get all the plans approved by not only the landlord who owned the commercial (that is, retail) space, but also from the board that managed the condo building (two separate approvals—let this be a lesson to avoid condo buildings, generally speaking, in any business endeavor). After four meetings with a scary guy named Jerry in midtown Manhattan and three iterations of architectural reviews, we finally got our approvals from them and signed the lease.

Now, however, as the clock was ticking to cut the hole, they were giving pushback. The condo management company said we needed approval again on this and they weren't giving it. I was pissed, this was absurd, it made no sense, we had the signatures needed, they had already approved this months prior, why give us such a hard time now?

I pushed and pushed my way into Jerry's office to get the re-approval; even the building manager was helping me out—we were down to the wire. It was December 18, and we had three days left of construction work before the holidays, before we were supposed to be done and moving in.

Mike the contractor called me.

"Helaine," he said, "We need to schedule the louver to be cut tomorrow or this isn't going to be done before the new year. What do you want to do?"

I was stressed, overwhelmed and far out of my comfort zone. But I realized I was chatting with someone who had been through this many times before, so I asked Mike what he would do if he were in my shoes, and he told me to call the building one more time to try to finalize the approval and call him back.

So, I called the building manager, whom I had struck a great relationship with. He was becoming my internal champion and we had gotten in the habit of chatting two to three times a day. He was an older, heavyset guy who always wore sweatpants, New Balance sneakers, and had an air of old New York about him.

"David, it's now or never," I implored him. "Jerry signed the plans last summer, so why is he putting up such a fight here and how do we move forward? If we don't do this now, we don't open, and we can't pay rent." I was trying to be strong but I was on the brink of tears. This was both of our issues, not just mine, and I wanted him to help be a part of the solution with me.

"Helaine, I know. I'm sorry," he said. "I wish there was something I could do. Maybe you should just cut the hole and ask for forgiveness later. You have the signed plans, and once it's cut, it's not like it could be uncut."

He laughed mischievously. This guy was amazing. Did he just tell me to cut the freaking hole? I think he did.

I sat on that for a while and then called our lawyer Jared. "Play this out with me," I instructed. We went through the risks of making this bold move, but because we'd gotten the initial approval, while there might be a legal back and forth, we had a good case.

An hour later, I called Mike. "Cut the hole tomorrow. Do it early and call me when it's over."

I remember intentionally sleeping in the next day, then going for a workout, avoiding heading down to the site until I got the call that the wall had been cut and the louver was being installed. I didn't know what was going to happen but I knew I had to take that risk, yet another big one, or we'd be done.

Two days later, I got a FedEx envelope at the studio, in which I was served with a legal notice from the building's lawyer. My hands shook as I read it, but there wasn't much substance and it never panned out. It just sat on my desk, proof that the risks get bigger and bigger but you have to just keep plowing forward.

Without that risky move, we wouldn't have opened in January (almost two years to the day of our first location opening) and who knows if we would have before the money and time ran out for CITYROW Upper East Side.

As if the louver incident wasn't enough, six weeks into opening the Upper East Side location, in the second week of February (during an exceptionally cold few days in NYC), one of the front desk closing emails on Saturday mentioned that one of the floor tiles (of our new $40,000-floor) in the basement was starting to come up.

Ugh, annoying, but we'll call the team on Monday to fix it.

The next morning, the phone starts ringing, and I learn that the entire studio floor is now more like an eighties-style waterbed. The four layers of cushion, rubber, plywood, and gym floor are moving like a lava lamp.

It turns out that after a below-freezing night in February, a pipe had burst in the condo building next door and their basement flooded. And since we share a floor with them, we were flooded too. There was six inches of water in the adjacent space, and our floor was ruined. The restoration guy came within a few hours, plucked up a tile and water came flowing out.

"I'm going to have to rip this whole thing out and get some fans in here to dry it out. It'll probably take four or five days for it to be fully dry."

"Do it," I said.

I recall being extremely calm and action-oriented. Shockingly I didn't cry, I just got to work to solve this urgent and important issue, starting to make calls to sort this out. I spoke to our lawyer, insurance broker, and construction team to rally around the best solutions. It was like when Jake and I were lost at sea—it was bad, we were definitely in crisis, but we'd get through it, so it was best to stay calm until we executed the plan.

For six weeks, we couldn't use our studio in our brand-new space. We had a tiny, five-person (as opposed to fifteen) room upstairs and could hold mini-classes, so we did. But this was a huge blow and would not enable us to grow this location.

~

We were just building momentum as a company, and everything above stifled our already weak grand opening. At the same time, there was no playbook for going from one to two studios and we'd missed a few things, mainly marketing and local studio awareness.

We expected that just like last time, we'd open our doors and people would flood in, especially with a retail location on the ground floor of a busy street. That didn't happen. This was a new location, new energy, and a new community we had to break into. We invested in some PR and subway ads to drum up some buzz, but it was a slog, and we needed to get to cash flow positive, quickly.

The end of 2016 going into 2017 was pretty bleak. After the basement flood, we tried to get our footing under us, and while insurance payments helped, we were a far cry from being cash flow-positive, and the fixed costs of the second location were causing us to burn money monthly. We had been cash flow-positive on month one of our first Union Square location, so we hadn't planned this kind of cash burn for the second location. We'd spent all our reserves on the buildout. It was so dire that we had to forego executive payroll (so, me and the other management members were making zero dollars) and make budget cuts while at the same time trying to grow the two locations into a cash flow-positive place. All the while knowing the second location, as overwhelming as it was now, was a piece of a larger vision and we had to get through this to keep building.

It was a grind—and definitely some of our darkest and hardest moments. We were far out of our comfort zones and skill sets. I doubted myself left and right. I succumbed to the big tears often and wondered if we'd get through this. I doubted myself more. On the flip side of the challenges we were facing, it was the year that we started to be recognized externally for the powerful brand we were creating. The bigger vision was coalescing, and that kept the fire inside us burning.

CHAPTER 7

RIPTIDES

D espite all the drama going on inside the company as we fought to keep it afloat, an outsider would never know. The classic "Instagram versus reality" was at play here. With all the PR and buzz around us and the fact that we were pioneering a completely new modality in fitness, we were starting to get noticed by companies looking to partner with us and people looking to bring CITYROW to a city near them. Tons of people started reaching out to ask if they could franchise. From the first email on, I laughed, thinking only of Subway or McDonalds, not our fancy boutique fitness studio. I filed them in an orange folder in my Gmail account and never even responded. Make your inbox work for you, right?

Then around the time we celebrated our first anniversary for the Upper East Side location, a few big franchise developers, rather than individuals, started reaching out. Out of curiosity, I responded to a couple of those emails, deciding that it couldn't hurt to learn about that world after all.

At first, I was very turned off by the various people I spoke with; they seemed slimy and disingenuous. But as one does when they're building, I started talking about the franchise opportunities and eventually in one of my networking events I was chatting with a friend and fellow Michigan grad, Dhani. We had just bonded over the fact that he had an idea to start a rowing company; his was going to be called "Strokes," and he enthusiastically went on and on about his business plan.

"Yeah, but you haven't actually done it yet—I did!" I told him, my bravado spiking. He laughed agreeably and said, "Seriously, though, if you're serious about franchising you gotta meet my guy, Jay."

"Meh," I said, already over franchising. I just didn't think premium boutique fitness had a place in the franchising world, but Dhani begged me to just take the call, and I finally agreed.

Right away, I realized there was something different about this franchise guy, Jay. He was authentic, real, and immediately got my vision about bringing a premium boutique fitness offering into the franchise world. He was impressed with what we'd built and we decided to continue the conversation. Now this was different and exciting.

Fast forward a year to 2018, a lot of legal fees, endless presentations compiling our entire business into a playbook—basically a quick PhD in franchising on my part—and we signed a deal to partner with Jay and his team based in Ann Arbor, MI to grow our retail operations (that is, our brick-and-mortar studios) nationally. We were officially franchisors! Outside of a small, $50,000 investment into the franchise entity (the company structure and backend), the only investment CITYROW had to make was in human capital, which we had plenty of—and we were fired up. This was also good because we didn't have any more reserves to invest in anything new. We were still trying to pay off our construction loan and get the Upper East Side location profitable.

We hit the ground running but our spirits were dampened a bit a few months in when we realized that there were also going to be some challenges becoming a franchisor, and especially that it was going to take a lot more capital than we'd originally budgeted.

First thing first, we had to open a test location/studio, which we decided to do in Michigan (home of my alma mater and our franchising partner) and had to turn around and figure out how to come up with the cost for it, which would be $200,000 or $300,000, minimum.

I, along with my co-founder Ashley, our head instructor Annie, and one of our advisors Jeff, decided to double down and we all turned over our 401Ks to fund this studio build-out, becoming franchisees ourselves (Fun fact: There's a special loophole in franchising where you can turn over your 401K into a franchise at zero penalty). We rounded things out with money from one of our CITYROW customers, and a personal investment from Dave, the new president of our franchising partner company. And that's how we got that local franchise business off the ground. We ran the process, opened the location, took all the learnings, and created a manual—a 180-page playbook—with every single detail on how to open a CITYROW franchise, right down to the type and size of the bathroom tiles and how far each mat is to be placed from each rower and where the artwork is hung in the lobby. No detail is too small.

As we continued to build our franchise brand, we started hosting "Discovery Days" for potential franchisees to learn about the business and, if there was a fit, buy one or more franchises.

Potential CITYROW franchisees came to Ann Arbor in the middle of summer, touring our still-under-construction studio with me, sat for a short presentation to introduce them to the brand, and then we all had dinner and drinks. The second day was a formal presentation, where they got to know more about us and the business mechanics.

Our franchise partner consisted of established "suits" who lifted me up, touting the amazing product we had built at CITYROW. It felt like they were also giving me an air of credibility and positive reinforcement that I had been lacking as a lonely founder for the prior four years. They gave us credit everywhere they could and told everyone who would listen that I was the product, driving the brand more than anyone or anything else could. I never had that level of external support and validation at CITYROW to help me recognize what I was bringing to the table. In normal jobs, you have bosses and checks and balances (hopefully), and now for the first time at CITYROW, I started to become really self-aware about what I brought to the table and when and where I needed to pat myself on the back. The potential franchisees wanted to learn about my entrepreneurial story. They couldn't get enough of CITYROW and our stories, fighting over who got to sit next to me at dinner, or one time, almost following me into the bathroom. Franchising is all about relationships, and building those came naturally to me. As a result, I *loved* the process.

One of our very first franchisees was a woman named Terri; we instantly connected. She had built her career in franchising and had been exploring finding the right fit for her (in terms of buying her own) for a really, really long time. When CITYROW finally hit the market, her broker brought it to her and it was love at first sight with the brand. When we met, she got it, because she had had her own back injuries like I had. I loved when people came to the table with their own stories of fitness and wellness. And like I said, it was all about relationships. When I met Terri, I thought to myself, "I think this woman is pretty cool, and it'd be fun to do some business with her."

She signed on and became our first official franchisee. Down the road as she approached opening, I recall vividly that her partner bought her a gold CITYROW necklace with a diamond and she was contemplating getting a CITYROW tattoo. I had neither of these things; she was possibly a bigger CITYROW fan than me. That was new—and a combination of shocking, exciting, and terrifying.

There was something about Discovery Days that gave me a different level of confidence from what I had been building over the years, side by side with the parts of me that were still damaged and carrying some of the weight from my childhood. I was the truest of insiders—suddenly, I was being touted as the best thing since sliced bread—and it felt good personally as well as what it meant for our company (and was the ultimate validation of our product and our brand). It wasn't just people telling me nice things or being written up in a popular magazine; it was people that we liked and respected embracing what we were doing, having done diligence on such a deep level that they were willing to commit their personal finances to it and dedicate their lives to building this brand alongside us. To me, that's the ultimate bet. However, this was also me, saying, *Oh my God, now I've got even more people that are riding this train and I need to make sure we're ready to keep going.*

It was an incredibly busy and fulfilling time. We were in the early days of building a strong franchise system and we couldn't wait to get our first units up and running across the country. At the same time, the pressure mounted on me with each new franchisee we welcomed into the CITYROW family.

Alongside franchising, we had also been thinking about an emerging angle on the digital side of fitness which was new, but potentially game-changing. I'd been watching the digital at-home fitness space and saw the early numbers coming out of Peloton. I thought it was the coolest thing I'd seen in years. Maybe, just maybe, we would build an app and a connected CITYROW rower.

I was then and will always be a tech fanatic—from the early days teaching Grandma how to use the computer to my corporate life to learning new systems and suggesting new ideas—and I just knew we (especially my co-founder Ashley whom I met at a tech company and who was as much of a tech junkie as I was) could create and deliver something special in that space. We *needed* to explore it.

In a catchup with my mentor and fellow entrepreneur and successful tech founder, Dan, he suggested we go hard into the digital world.

Why? Well, we had a unique and competitive advantage in the market because I, alongside Ashley, were fitness founders with a background in tech, something that is not common. In fact, tech was our expertise. We had an edge there and we'd built a strong fitness product, so Dan felt, and soon enough I felt, that we should take a big swing.

Once again, creativity and problem-solving had to come into play, now more than ever. We were eking by in the two corporate NYC studios, but just barely. I was able to steadily raise more angel capital based on our franchise deal (first impending then signed) and the new impetus for digital. Now our vision was starting to come into focus. It felt good and right—in my gut I was nervous about adding any more to my plate, but I knew this was our destiny.

We were building a national brand that dominated both brick and mortar as well as the budding at-home sector.

Here we go—*this* is what we set out to do, what we'd build to change the industry. It was a lot, I was overwhelmed, but it all started to click and the path forward was clearer than ever. The fitness world was becoming fragmented between at-home and in-person and we'd not only bridge the gap, but show people a way to see results regardless of where they wanted to work out. We would cycle consumers between both extensions of the brand, leading to stronger business economics overall. Boom.

My confidence was building and the vision was tightening up into something I could see and feel; more importantly, it was also being received well by others. We started to plan the execution across all sectors and it was thrilling, terrifying, humbling, and exhausting all at the same time.

Then I landed a huge spot on the *Today* show. It was a segment on women in business and it was a profile, getting interviewed by the one and only Savannah Guthrie. It included a sit down, a tour of the Upper East Side location, and then Savannah (and Al Roker) would take a class. According to our PR contact, "we'd peaked" with this segment. Apparently, it didn't get any better than that.

It was a high, a moment in the CITYROW journey that will stick with me forever. For the stress leading up, the outfit choices, the prep, the people we had to recruit to stage the mid-day class—including my mom and a childhood friend who was a huge *Today* show fan (and luckily kept her cool)—to my co-founder being so pregnant she should not have been working so hard, let alone hustling behind the scenes to make the day happen. And then came the magic of the actual piece, which encapsulated the essence of the story and what we were building. It aired a week later and Annie,

Ashley, and I sat drinking mimosas and watching and cheering for ourselves, because it was a win, a big one.

You have to celebrate the wins large and small and sit in them, because they balance out the lows and the tears.

It was more than a fluff piece, as it highlighted our new franchise offering and the upcoming app launch. It turns out that the *Today* show nailed storytelling. We not only sold franchises based on that piece alone but the momentum grew in the investor world as well.

Until then, I had been hustling angel investors and those who understood our omnichannel vision, those that got us, and those who were a quick close. However, for larger groups of institutional investors, we just didn't fit into many of their models and it was a long, exhausting grind every time I went out to do a bigger fundraise with the same result: No.

Personally, it was a confusing time as a founder and CEO. Things were really starting to flow and our strategy was unique and powerful, but it wasn't landing with institutional investors. At this point, the business was bigger and we really needed a larger capital partner to fuel both the franchise and digital sides. So, I doggedly kept at the long and hard search for a large institutional investor.

Through a friend of a friend, I landed a meeting with the principal of an early-stage venture capital who also happened to row in college. Instead of the interest and support I expected, without listening to a word I said, let alone letting me finish the pitch (forget bothering to get to know our vision, strategy, and traction), he ripped the business apart. "No one is ever going to want to row," he said, then continued to go on and on.

He eventually tossed the business plan I'd carefully printed out and collated back to me across the table. "That model is simply not going to work. You can't do both digital and brick and mortar." He added things like, "The footprint is too small" and "These businesses cannibalize each other." He kept going for the remainder of the hour as to why this wasn't going to work, barely asking a question or letting me offer a friendly rebuttal.

He took a bite of his blueberry scone and smiled pleasantly, having no idea he'd just destroyed my day, my week. At the time, I just didn't have the language or the framework yet to fire back at him. I didn't have the years under me to realize he'd never even *built* a business, only analyzed them. I knew he was wrong and clearly not someone who could see, let alone appreciate, change, but back then it was easy to let my fears and insecurities take over, and I wanted to crawl into the floorboards and disappear. I sobbed in the back of the yellow cab on the way back to the office, but by the time the ride was over, I was calm, with makeup reapplied, and ready to greet the CITYROW team.

It seemed that everything we were doing—as ambitious as it was and with as much buzz as we were generating—still didn't fit the institutional investors' thesis: CITYROW was brick and mortar, plus hardware, plus software. Most funds' thesis were one, maybe two, but never all three of those. I was frustrated. I was mad. I was sad. I blamed myself for not being able to accomplish the task at hand. However, I knew we were onto something, so channeled everything I could into plowing forward.

I had too many experiences like that former-rower/investor. In fact, they represent most of the end results of most investor meetings I had from 2015 to 2021, but as they say, it only takes one. You have to (and will) get hundreds of No's before the life-changing Yes.

Because then there were times like when I was visiting a long-distance friend in LA who'd been watching me build the business over the years and who was a founder himself. I dropped by his place for brunch, he made some amazing enchiladas, and we smoked some great weed. By the time we'd reminisced, caught up on business, and finished our meal, he'd signed documents and wired six figures into the CITYROW account without even laying eyes on our financials or a business plan.

"Is this really happening," I whispered to my friend, whom I'd called while waiting for my Lyft outside his massive house in Santa Monica, "or am I just really stoned?!"

Yes, there were some bright spots of killer angels who bet on us during those years, like my friend in Santa Monica, and many more friends and former co-workers, but we really needed that big infusion of capital so I could focus on execution and not the constant fundraise cycle. So, we decided to think outside the box. If traditional institutions weren't working, but we were growing and would continue to grow both in physical studios and digital, we could go after a strategic partner, WaterRower. They were our manufacturing partner for the custom CITYROW rowing machines we were building for our digital/at-home business and the provider of rowers of our studio locations. Basically, we would ask them to invest money in the company to fund the operations alongside being the hardware component of our brand. We had an established manufacturing relationship, but this would take everything to a much bigger level all around.

We first brought the idea to the number two person at the company over a casual living room strategy session. He was into the concept and we ideated, brainstormed, and dreamed of what this would look like. It was synergistic and made sense. The question was, could we get the WaterRower CEO on board, knowing it was not his bread and butter? The ask was $1 million, not a small chunk of change (and by far the largest investment we'd had to date), but also still relatively small in the grand scheme of VC investments.

We worked on a proposal for months and eventually I went up to the WaterRower headquarters in Rhode Island with my part-time chief financial officer, Jeff, a fifty-something guy (one of the ones in a blazer who showed up to help me many times). As we started pitching and discussing the mechanics of the deal with the CEO, it was clear he just wanted to hear from Jeff. The meeting progressed and I quickly realized the role I was here to play was the founder, the product, the visionary, but when it came to finances and investments, Jeff needed to lead the charge to get our points across.

I would process this later and go through some emotions of frustration, anger, and disappointment, and ultimately make peace with the fact that in sales you have to give your client what they need to feel comfortable to get the deal done, sexism aside. This is the reality of business. In this instance, the CEO knew and liked me but to get the deal done, we had to put Jeff at the forefront. No wonder women get so frustrated at every turn trying to raise money and build companies. This needs to change immediately if not sooner.

Despite our challenges, we put the right people in for the play at the right time and it paid off. After lots of back and forth trying to make a deal between a legacy manufacturer and a tech company, we finally got to an investment plan. It was unconventional and not a straight equity deal like we had hoped for (that mechanism didn't work for their business model) but through ultimately structuring the investment as a loan, we got the deal done. We were officially partners and we had $1 million in the bank. Time to put our heads down and launch our digital product!

We spent the next eight months after that meeting building and structuring the digital business. It was a big undertaking, yet parts were familiar to us—especially for Ashley and me, as we'd been here before, building tech—so there was an ease to it that was contradictory to the brick-and-mortar side of the business.

We hired an outside agency to work on the app, and had MacGyvered our studio in NYC to start filming content for the app between classes twice a week. In other words, we were learning on the fly, being scrappy, and quickly had our MVP (minimum viable product), which was an iOS app with on-demand CITYROW classes, ready to start beta testing with customers who already had their own rowers at home.

From there it was time to launch our first custom rower (a Bluetooth-enabled rower to sync our customers' data, something that we learned was important to the at-home athlete or workout buff) and start working on our second rower, or what we were at first calling V2. It would be a fully interactive rower with a touchscreen and other amazing bells and whistles.

As we approached a year into the digital build, with the mvp in hand and hundreds of strong beta customer reviews, it was time to market this new product. Naturally at this point in a start-up, it was time to raise money. We needed cash, and I was faced with having to raise another $1.5 million, a process that I was dreading as if it were my execution. I'd been burned and burned and burned and burned and burned and burned. Also, with no success in the typical pathways to capital, I was discouraged. I didn't know where else to turn with all my previous No's (my failures); WaterRower had made it clear they didn't want to or plan to fund anything at CITYROW beyond the initial $1 million tranche.

But WaterRower had taught me that strategic partnerships could be successful when positioned correctly, so I decided to try my luck at what was successful previously—going to our other big partner, our franchising partner, and explaining where we were.

Initially, they'd completely discouraged the idea of me forming a digital arm to the company. "Don't do that," they advised sternly. "It will ruin the franchise business."

But eventually, we got them to see it as a powerful strength, one that would make us a cutting-edge franchise system (them included), pioneers in the franchise world, noticed for embracing change and innovation. They finally jumped into our corner and invested in the digital build with us.

Our franchising partner knew WaterRower had seeded the initial digital investment. When we shared with them the plan to raise another $1.5 million, and our desire to have all our strategic partners aligned on the cap table (where they share the same upside when we were acquired or sold), they expressed interest in joining the parent company in a larger way.

After a handful of conversations between Discovery Days in Ann Arbor, Jay (the head of our franchising partner) mentioned that they were going to raise funds on their own and would want to take on our whole round of funding under that umbrella.

That was music to my ears, because while we struggled to fit into institutional funds' boxes, our partners would continue to join forces in larger ways—being our investment partners—and there is no bigger vote of confidence. I took the words at face value from a partner whom I'd shaken hands with before. I exhaled, smiled, and went back to executing, so thrilled I didn't have to go out to fundraise. It was July and we'd made it clear that October was our cash-out date (that is, the day we would run out of money and when we needed more in the bank) so we'd work toward that.

I didn't create a backup plan. These were our partners. I'd seen success there before and assumed that there was no way it would fall apart. I didn't want to believe it wouldn't happen.

Big mistake. Huge.

As the months wore on, I followed up to move this along, get a term sheet, get aligned on those terms, and start the diligence process, but the closing date for the money kept getting moved forward into the future. I should have seen the red flags—but they were amazing humans and partners. In fact, they were such great partners that when we reached that drop-dead date that fall as the deal dragged on, two of them wired personal funds to cover payroll and keep the company afloat until it got done. I admired this move so much and hoped to be that person for another company one day.

In retrospect, I was so blinded by the thought that we'd repeat the strategic partnership deal and I wouldn't have to go out yet again and try to find a needle in a haystack. I didn't ask the right questions. I didn't push the right buttons. I didn't actually get a term sheet done as quickly as I should have. I put every single one of my eggs in that basket and just forged ahead, dragging the basket with me, not worrying if any of the eggs were cracking.

Meanwhile, the company was running on fumes.

It got to a point where the term sheet and money still were nowhere in sight. As it turned out, the higher-ups at our franchising partner company had over-promised and under-delivered on this new area of business for them within their funding arm. They were still in the process of raising it themselves, and were new to it. Once again, as great partners, two of them ended up writing CITYROW two *more* personal checks to cover *more* payroll. But the bigger funding issue was still outstanding.

With those personal checks, we had runway to make payroll, but we weren't able to pay any of our vendor payables, which were massive because we were in the midst of launching our first rower that fall and had a lot of upfront cash to outlay. Our vendor bills started to quickly creep up (reminiscent of our UES construction build) and it was also embarrassing to be the client that couldn't pay. Despite how hard I pushed and how many times I called for an update, eventually as the new year approached, our credit cards got cut off. This was rock bottom. I still had no term sheet for the money promised by the franchising partner, and panic set in. I frantically tried to figure out what the hell was happening. I knew in my gut they wanted to do this deal, so what was going on?

I remember going to a friend's house for dinner that January and feeling like this was it, it had to be over. I'd failed. We had no money for payroll, our credit card were shut off, we owed so many great vendors payables. And the plan we had was falling apart. My friends tried to talk me through it but even I, a constant optimist and creative problem solver and the little engine that could, was out of gas.

Finally, *finally*, after weeks of me tearing my hair out trying to find a replacement partner, Jay called and said they'd found an incredible partner to do this deal in place of them, a family office, and connected me with them. And while an equity deal had been on the table with our franchising partner for the last eight months, the family office they connected me to was ready to... give us a loan.

My heart sank. That wasn't going to work.

We already had a debt partner, WaterRower. As we went to the table to figure out how to make this new loan partnership work, the urgency of payroll and the Amex shut-off was real, so we quickly did a deal with them for a bridge loan for $500,000 (while we worked on a bigger investment plan). That bridge quickly went out the door to cover the past four months of vendors and execution. Now we had six weeks to get a larger deal done with the family office. It wasn't a solution; it was only a band-aid that at best bought us a short amount of time.

We got in the weeds with this family office, both sides hungry to get a deal done, to remove the bridge loan and start executing together. However, we immediately ran into another block, a big one. I knew it. The fact that we already had a senior debt holder—WaterRower—meant that this family office would not be able to get first position, and WaterRower wouldn't move down the stack. "First position" in these kinds of loan scenarios is important because it means the entity in that position gets paid back first no matter what happens (good or bad) by way of a company liquidation.

Weeks of frantic calls trying to get either party to take the second position fell flat. The deal was falling apart because of a prior deal's terms. These are the tiny but hugely important things that most people are unaware of that can sometimes sink a company, or at least bring a founder to her limit.

Without a deal, we were left with an overpriced bridge loan with a crazy interest rate (it was never meant to be long-term), along with all our other loans (to WaterRower and the franchising partner company's founders who'd written personal check loans), also with crazy interest rates, and two weeks of runway to find another capital partner. It was impossible. We were fucked. It was April. We'd run out of cash that prior January and were days away from a repeat scenario.

I was personally at the end of my rope: those first few months of 2019 took a toll on me and I wasn't sure I could do it again.

It was a confusing dichotomy to live in because on the flip side, we were selling franchises like crazy. And we had the only connected rower in the market. Things were growing. But we had no money—not even credit cards. It was shameful; I was embarrassed, angry, frustrated, and confused. Naturally, I blamed myself and based that on what I was doing wrong, or at least what I *perceived* I was doing wrong.

I was out of options that spring and knew that two weeks was not a feasible timeline to approach the VC market from scratch, so I had to go back to WaterRower—to Peter, the CEO, who by then felt like Daddy Warbucks. I walked into his office with my tail between my legs because I knew he never intended or wanted to be our bank. He would see this as my personal failure to raise outside capital. Now I was basically putting him in a position to either put more money in or take over the company. He didn't want either.

Either way, he had all the leverage. I knew this was our only shot at keeping the company going so I had to accept whatever terms might be offered. It was a shitty place and a hopeless feeling. After weeks of hard conversations where I couldn't hold back my tears, he reluctantly funded CITYROW with another $1 million, saving the business, but also in the process negotiating 50 percent of the digital side of the business, taking for himself half of what was becoming the most valuable part of the overall business. It was not a good deal, especially for me and our early employees. In fact, it sucked, there's no other word for it. But it was that or shut down, and as Simon Sinek touts in *The Infinite Game*, "You have to survive to win." We did what we had to do to survive. And I'd do it again, because we had to. Ask any founder what deals they had to do to survive and most will have a story—or many stories—like this.

Those were some of the worst months ever, figuring out how we were going to get through it all personally and professionally. That second million from WaterRower wasn't getting us nearly as far as we needed it to go. We were growing and needed to invest to continue the growth, which meant we were burning money at every turn (but the growth was working, so we had to add more fuel to the fire!). Before that funding hit the bank, I was already thinking about a next round of capital.

Franchising was poised to be profitable, but we wouldn't see that profit until the studios were themselves operating profitably for a while.

On the digital side of things, we were starting to advertise, and at the same time, build out the second machine, fully integrated and gorgeous. That business was set to burn cash for a while—a big digital swing took a lot of capital—and it would also be a while before franchising could cash flow to support that side of the business.

At this point, the summer of 2019, we had our first seven franchises preparing to open, and were selling more every month. Our digital products were in market and steadily gaining traction, so I was able to level-up our fundraise to attract some big angels off that momentum. We started getting crisper in articulating our vision, telling our game-changing, holistic omnichannel brand story and it started resonating. Conversations with potential investors were going better than they ever had before and at the same time, and we started posting some decent revenue numbers as both business units grew.

High level, regardless of how you get it in the bank, the second you take outside capital, it's like you're on a highway—the more money you raise and the faster you raise it, the faster and bigger you need to go. You have to pretend like you're in a shiny F1 race car in front of investors, potential investors, the media, even your staff, when in reality, the road is only being built as you drive, mere inches in front of you. You're running out of gas, you have whiplash at every turn, and the car is falling apart under you.

I'm not sure how I kept going through all those years of never quite achieving the big fundraise I was constantly striving for and dealing with all the small and huge problems along the way. Looking back, it's one big blur with the rollercoaster of running out of money becoming the unfortunate norm. Little did I know that 2014-2019 was child's play compared to what 2020 would bring.

My personal life had a baseline stress mimicking that of CITYROW. I went months/years without a salary (fortunate to be able to rely on family support) and I both resented myself for it and felt guilty that I was able to hang on because of that support. Here I was, a capable, strong, badass businesswoman who needed to be supported by her family. I was grateful and appreciative, of course, and it was maybe okay in the very beginning, but when it kept happening "Grandma," I would say, red-faced and in a small voice very much unlike my own, "Can you help me cover rent this month?", it really eroded my confidence and energy, and took a toll on me. There wasn't much left over for me to do, like build a personal life, much less financial security.

But I didn't feel like I had a choice except to keep going. This was the company I started, with my friends who'd become family and people who bet on me and put money on it. I was going to give it everything.

CHAPTER 8

THE TSUNAMI

Going into 2020, we were firing on all cylinders. I remember on New Year's Eve (going into that year), I stepped away from the party I was at, looked out the window at the moon, and manifested with all my might for the upcoming year, knowing that it was going to be THE year that all our hard work started to pay off. It was time to explode this concept and let the rocket ship soar.

With franchising, we were weathering the storm of our first few operational learnings, preparing for the next wave of grand openings, dealing with new and unforeseen challenges left and right, and at the same time, working hard to sell more franchises, with a new structure that would be slower, but more economical for the brand at its current level of maturity.

It was an unbelievable amount of stimulating work getting this new business lane off the ground and giving it our all to drive success. We built so many presentations and there were still so many more to do. The pressure was on for the overall business (NYC studios, the franchises, and the digital combined), but also to support the amazing people who had bet on CITYROW to be a part of their present but, most importantly, their future.

As the second and then third wave of franchise openings were coming up, we started to get our feet under us and finally, the two openings slated for March and April 2020 beat all pre-sales records at any of our studios by a landslide. I was insanely proud of our franchisees and couldn't wait to apply the learnings to the next phase of growth. Royalties and profitability were right on the horizon.

On the digital side, our first app had launched over two years before, with dozens of on-demand CITYROW rowing classes of different lengths and variety. It was still our MVP, marketed primarily to those who already have their own machines. But we had this strong product in market and the word was spreading, subscriptions were ticking up, and we watched as the monthly subscription revenue grew. Then our branded CITYROW Classic rowing machine entered the market in late 2018, and we were on the map with the first-ever at-home rowing content. We were also well on our way to a bigger launch of our souped-up, fully integrated (with a fancy touchscreen tablet and all) new machine in the fall of 2020.

In our New York City studios, things were humming along on one hand, but not growing so much—only one was profitable on a unit-economics basis. That was bad. We needed strong management there but struggled to find someone to really own and grow the locations. With Ashley and I focused on growth, this fell down the priority list. We went through many managers; frankly, our budget and resources were focused on growth in franchising and digital so the studios did get the shaft of attention at times; yet, it was the show pony where we entertained people and welcomed franchisees and potential investors, so it had to be in good shape and run well. Ultimately, it was a big time and energy suck that took a toll on the team.

It's a lot going from a one-location boutique fitness business to a growing company where we're a franchisor and a pioneer in digital. Our vision of an omnichannel approach held firm—these were all complementary businesses. But it was a shit ton to manage, made that much harder with the ongoing limited capital. We finally found a great operator to come in and build up our NYC studios—we were going to overpay a little—but you have to invest in growth, right?

Then in March 2020, COVID-19 hit and the world as we knew it came to an abrupt halt.

It was an absolute blur. Information—or the lack thereof—was coming fast and furious, and we didn't know what to do.

The earliest days were a roller coaster of thoughts, emotions, and trying to balance clients, employees, and a growing global pandemic that was so uncertain. Do we close our NYC studios, our home base, or do we stay open? Initially, we (and many other boutiques) thought that people would need a physical outlet for their mental health, because this shit was stressful. But we had our finger on the pulse, listening and learning, and on the morning of Sunday, March 15, we were committed to staying open. But by two in the afternoon, we found ourselves in a mad dash to close down, get communications out, and stay connected with our staff and clients.

I was so stressed with closing the studios I didn't even realize I had COVID myself until I lost my taste and smell.

Once the decision was made to close the studios, it was all about figuring out what the hell to do now. We needed and wanted to do everything we could to best support our clients and staff—that was our biggest concern. How were we going to pay our staff with no studios open? What would happen to our franchisees? Everyone was stuck at home, that was bad. Could we help them in some way? Was there a way to be the answer people needed as an outlet at this time?

Given our digital expertise (and the fact that unlike a lot of companies that scrambled at the onslaught of COVID to get an at-home product up and running, we were already in market), we saw a window and pivoted to online content. Right away we started doing live classes on Instagram and shared our app widely, with new bodyweight-only, no-rower-needed classes. It was what our community needed. When possible, we (and many of our franchisees) let clients borrow rowers and weights from our studios. We were in the thick of managing through it ourselves, while also immediately needing to have a strong POV to lead our franchisees. It was a true shit show every which way—the rules differed by city and state, and our locations were scattered across the country. We did our best and it never felt like enough. It was the wild west out there and we just needed to survive to see another day. Adversity wasn't new to me and this company, so while it was a tsunami we never saw coming, we were no stranger to this position. With so many challenges under our belt, this was just another, bigger obstacle. There was confidence beneath the fear, knowing we could and would get through anything; we had done it before.

On the flip side, orders for our rower and sign-ups for our app flew in, and a good (potential) problem became whether WaterRower could keep up with the manufacturing demand for the machines. We're proud of the fact that our rowers are manufactured in the US, but they had a relatively small team and were starting to see COVID outbreaks on the factory floor. I'd never worried about manufacturing before but now it was all we talked about. Luckily, WaterRower handled this exceptionally well and prioritized our orders. We never got past a four-week ship window.

The gym/fitness studio world had been flipped over and dumped out, and the press was hungry for content and commentary. Our PR consultant made sure we were right there, speaking, weighing in, and providing insight and workouts—giving anything to both keep the CITYROW brand alive and provide people stuck at home with engaging ways to move. We had a unique perspective, having a foot in both studios and digital, so outlets were hungry for our POV.

Those early days of COVID were scary and unnerving but also riveting and creative. As a company, we pivoted and made about a thousand tactical changes overnight.

The looming tsunami—so few people can handle getting hit by a big wave, much less running right at it. That's what we did. I'm incredibly proud of how we handled those insane (or as it was described then, unprecedented) weeks.

It was a global tragedy and while we had to navigate being in the midst of one of the largest disasters in our lifetimes, for us at CITYROW, I can also say that those days brought up and out some of the most compelling energy and best traits we had as a team. Of course, it was creative problem-solving and resilience, but it was also looking fear in the eye and seeing opportunities where other people saw closed doors.

The question in those days was, will you survive or die? I decided we were going to survive, at all costs, and I would steamroll over everything to make this happen. The decision to keep going forces you to keep thinking outside the box, because there's almost always a rabbit to pull out of the hat if you look hard and long enough.

It went far beyond survival. We decided we were going to take everything that was happening—and this massive demand for at-home fitness—and grow and thrive. I had a fresh fire in my belly from battling 2020 and was ready to bring that energy into the fundraising world yet again. This time I wouldn't stop until we had more than enough capital to execute on the full omnichannel vision.

I was going to have my work cut out for me.

Amidst the massive impact of COVID on the company, I was introduced via our franchising partner to an investor named Arie and we totally hit it off. We had a series of phone calls and he was no stranger to brick and mortar, loved tech, and immediately got the omnichannel vision (for once, someone embraced the online and offline combination!). He was eager to get involved and help us lead a round of funding and do some backend business cleanup to prepare for another, bigger one.

He and I met in a random suburban parking lot in early June—eager for an IRL (in real life) meetup, but still social distancing.

Arie had amazing complementary skill sets to me; he taught me more about company structures, governance, and boards of directors. He pushed (well, more like shoved) me out of my comfort zone and helped me reorganize the business so it was more attractive to institutional investors, and set up a board. He got his hands dirty and ultimately led a crucial round for CITYROW during that first COVID summer, which gave us the capital to see us through both the crazy growth on the digital side along with the decimation of our franchises and studios.

When you find the right investor and partner, it just flows, and that's what happened with Arie. A thousand No's and then the right alignment happens. It took me six years but I found it—a great partnership and the right amount of capital.

Even with the capital raise with Arie and the structure work that went along with it, though, we still had a ton of execution to do, within the confines of a global pandemic. We were in a decent place on digital but didn't yet have enough capital to invest heavily, despite great economics and a strong supply chain (thank you again, American-made rowers). Where we weren't in a decent place: our new franchise system. Those record-breaking grand openings obviously never happened and the studios just ramping up were cut off at the knees. It was devastatingly painful, it hurt me deeply to see our franchisees suffering, yet I had to put on a very brave face. The untold story is all those behind-the-scenes tears after an all-hands call. These were my *people*, they loved this brand as much as I did, if not more, and they were being pummeled by the covid waves, with few ways to come up for air.

In July 2020, I was out in Colorado and went to visit Terri, our very first franchisee whom I'd really hit it off with at the start of that part of the CITYROW journey. We had coffee and through tears she told me she had to close the studio she'd only opened six months before. And though she was stuck with a Small Business Association loan, she couldn't see a world where she could reopen and relaunch when the time came and COVID restrictions were lifted.

There were many other stories like this, painful ones, ones that broke my heart. Just like those franchisees dreamed of owning a business, I'd dreamed of watching and supporting them grow, but COVID knocked the legs out from under all of us.

I did my best to stay positive and innovative, to be strong for the team, our partners, and franchisees, but it was draining and uncertain. I was feeling the strain on my hard-fought-for confidence.

At the same time our franchises were crumbling, all that digital work we did for CITYROW in 2017 and 2018 paid off and the tailwinds we were riding on that front saved the business in the short term (and we knew studios would come back, eventually). Over the holidays that year, we did really well. Unfortunately, that was immediately followed by cash flow issues yet again (finding the right timing on future payables is another business lesson to learn), and I had to (yet again) hold executive team payroll, and do a quick fundraising raise from our top investors to (yet again) buy myself a few months.

We needed a big raise to support this huge digital upswing and we didn't have a big window of time. We had to take advantage of the opportunity to grow when people were stuck at home. But at this point, I didn't know where to start. We didn't have an institutional lead investor on board yet (Arie was our guardian angel investor but he was only one person, not a whole fund of his own) who could quickly fund this rocket ship, and time was of the essence. I needed to change things up and I needed (more) help.

By that point, I was living down in Miami, and a visiting friend, who knew about my struggles with fundraising but also really believed in me, wanted me to meet his boss, who was, he said, a fundraising machine.

I was reluctant. As much as I knew we needed to go outside of my network, and bring new energy into the mix, it was still hard to imagine trusting someone to actually get this done alongside me. I'd engaged with many parties who'd fallen flat at fundraising. But this fellow founder and I hit it off, vibing and riffing.

It was the turning point in the company's fundraising trajectory.

He was a hustler, so we spoke the same language fluently. He was ready to get on board, to the point where on the spot he sold his Concept 2 rower (a competitor of ours) and then bought a CITYROW machine, all during our breakfast of eggs and toast.

This guy was in fact an incredible fundraiser, with a proven track record across several companies. He told me he'd help raise a quick bridge round of funding, then do a Series A—which was our next-level north star round of funding—alongside me, in exchange for a seat on the board of directors I'd begun creating. Let's fucking go.

Then, I witnessed the magic.

Within seventy-two hours, we raised almost $2 million from his network. Via text messages. It was surreal—this guy was my hero.

He had an ability to communicate the crux of a fundraising pitch faster and more concise than anyone I'd ever met. He nailed the CITYROW opportunity and value prop in 140 characters or less.

I immediately put that capital to work, working in the trenches with him to drive growth and plan for a quick larger round that would give us the capital to go big across all our sectors and truly bring the omnichannel vision to life. The at-home fitness market was white hot and Peloton was valued at $8 billion. This was our time.

He opened the doors and I closed the deals. It was great to have a new partner on the fundraising side, someone with complementary skill sets to facilitate the right conversations, setting me up with the right people, and then letting me do my thing. I really learned then that this is the right dynamic for me (and most young founders): someone who not only believed in me, but also trusted me to deliver. It helped feed my confidence and made me feel less alone.

Quickly after the bridge round, with his help, I raised $12 million from three strong VC funds and a handful of rockstar (I'm talking big) angels. I went from literally not being able to afford to pay my staff (much less myself) to a company flush with cash in a matter of three months.

TechCrunch (the Bible of the tech world) covered the raise. It felt like we were on top of the world. Every investor reached out to congratulate me. Friends who'd watched us since day one couldn't believe it. I was booked for interviews left and right, and it felt like we were in a new stratosphere of start-ups. More money, more visibility, more pressure.

Then there was just one last thing to do: celebrate. We had to recognize this win, this big win, and this amazing milestone for the company. Putting my fears (especially around the bigger risks we were taking as a company and would continue to have to take) aside for one day, and a fun night, and just sit in this moment of triumph. The future was scary and uncertain but we'd worked hard, very hard, for seven whole years for this milestone. While my temptation was to turn right around and continue to work, we took a time out and partied hard that night.

CHAPTER 9

SETTING SAIL

When we finally achieved our Series A milestone, not only did we smash it (got it in the door quickly, with a crazy-high company valuation), but we raised from people that I was excited to partner with. These investors were the real deal, and their job (some being on the board, and some investing a lot of straight cash) was to help us succeed by way of support in any way they could.

The immediate aftermath of the Series A closing was a combination of elation (We finally did the thing we'd been working toward for years!) and some fear (Holy shit, time to execute, I hope we can deliver!) and excitement (Hell, yeah, we finally get to go do the thing we've been dreaming of!)—and we, *finally*, won't have to worry about payroll. It's our *time* to build everything we've been talking about and strategizing on. Our biggest blocker was eliminated, the future was *ours*!

We finally started executing on some exciting projects—to grow both our physical and digital footprints, increase our content, and build out our tech capabilities. The energy across the company was tingly, like we'd been waiting to get on that big ride at Disney World and were finally seeing what all the fuss was about. I watched the team shine and grow, flex new muscles, and build things smarter and better than we'd even dreamed. There were some really incredible things we did, built, and invested in, in those months coming off the raise.

For a time, it was fantastic. I really, really thought that raising that capital was the single thing that was going to magically solve a lot of our challenges and enable us to break into the next phase of the business. After all, it had been the biggest goal on my (and our team's) professional agenda for seven years. I've been fixating on fundraising for so long that when it happened, I imagined it would be the biggest unlock, enabling me and CITYROW to cruise, or at least take a few deep breaths.

I misjudged that. Severely. Because when the capital problem was seemingly solved, so many more company challenges, blocked by the money issue for the better part of a decade, surfaced. It made sense. We had a big backlog of needs on the sidelines, waiting for the capital that had to be attended to, so that when there finally *was* capital, everything and everyone showed up with hands out to be solved or paid.

With so much team energy used manually plugging holes and keeping the company together with duct tape, gum, and a hairclip over the years, we now had a lot of cleanups to do to turn that duct-taped skeleton into a stable structure that was primed for long, strong growth.

It's true that all companies experience growing pains, and that's often exacerbated when they're handed huge amounts of money overnight and pushed to grow quickly. CITYROW was no different. Now that we had this money, we were speeding faster, careening ever more aggressively on the highway in our shiny sports car, and new things started to break—big things, things that shouldn't break on a new car, like having to replace seemingly capable drivers for being asleep at the wheel mid-journey. Or like having the wheels come off.

Human resources broke. The decent infrastructure across platforms (things like processes and systems for getting things done) that we thought we had established was not enough. It wasn't strong enough for our new needs. As we catapulted, our ability to project-manage fell flat, because we went from four to five big projects at a time to fifteen to twenty, some of which were ten times the size, like our whole website overhaul or building a brand-new production studio in the heart of Midtown Manhattan.

I've since learned that often things need to break to be rebuilt in a better, stronger way (and this goes for me personally too), but when things break, people, projects, clients, and employees suffer. Over and over, I blamed myself for the breaks. Especially as a female leader—we're harder on ourselves than our male counterparts, that's for sure—it's important to acknowledge and remember that things breaking is par for the course. In start-ups, it's very normal. Unfortunately I didn't have this perspective at the time and I personally carried the weight of every crack and every break.

Today, when things go wrong in business or in any way in my life, I tell myself, *Don't be so hard on yourself, Helaine.* Then, in the thick of breakage everywhere at the pinnacle of our trajectory, it was harder to do.

Technology had become the core of our business: we were creating a connected/digital rower...and our technology broke. It broke in a big way, due to the shakiness of our infrastructure, not having the right people on the tech side, trying to build versus buy off the shelf, and a lack of management accountability—something I must and will always own as the CEO and leader. Your team's failures are your failures, so hire well! This miss was the vehicle that caused a cascading effect across the company. Contributing to all of it was failed communication across the board, which again is all on me and I own 100 percent. I wasn't close enough to to the tech side of the business (when I should have been) to know that we were building our own answer to e-commerce from scratch—not a good idea for a company trying to grow on so many fronts—when we should have used Shopify and saved ourselves a huge number of headaches. As the CEO and leader, I should have made sure that everything was out in the open and accountability was at the forefront in every part of the company, and with every person. Communication is key and mandatory, everywhere and with everyone, no matter if the communication is good, bad, or ugly. You gotta do it.

As a founder and builder (and a female), I'm always going to see the tarnishes before the glow—it's part of what pushes forward growth and drives us to perfection—but as I look back, I still see so much of the shine. Between the dropped balls and mis-judgements, incredible things still happened. We built a world-class production facility to shoot our CITYROW content and classes in record time in the heart of NYC. We launched live classes. We were going to go from shooting *ten* classes a week to *forty-five* classes a week, and were recruiting to level-up our instructor base. We started updating our website and our infrastructure. We absolutely delighted our customers and clients. We were set to do all the things that we had been talking about doing for so long. It was really fucking cool in so many ways, and despite working through a new world and a new set of challenges, we were still on a high.

I really believed we were doing the best job out there in connected fitness, had the best team, had the best product, and had the potential to be even better. In my mind, with money, now we had it all. I thought we were going to be immune to some of the classic start-up or fast-growth challenges because I knew they would probably come, and felt we were prepared for them.

Nope, we were not.

And all the things that broke were devastating, in part because it's always devastating when things break. That's life. But personally, I really thought we'd avoid some of them because I'd studied this world, the phases, the steps it would take, and knowledge is power, right? But the thing I know now is that you can't always know what's coming next, even with the best team, best investors, best board.

The beauty is, always has been, and always will be, not in the preparation or the dreaming but in the rebuild, the pivots, and the rising from the ashes.

So, in those failures, alongside some really big wins, we learned that we were just a start-up that had to go through the same series of waves that everyone else had to face. It was, in a word, humbling.

Personally, it was a very emotional time. I had to balance the feeling of being proud of this big accomplishment and milestone that thrust CITYROW and me as the leader into the spotlight, not to mention the attention we were getting for pioneering omni-channel fitness, and also deal with the most challenging business, human, and operational challenges I'd ever faced. I was bouncing back and forth, faster than ever, between success and failure. It's a common feeling for founders to feel like failures, and I forced myself to listen carefully to founder friends who'd been here before, and remind myself over and over that all of us feel that way (maybe more often than not), and I was no different.

Then there were the large, macroeconomic factors brewing in the world, and especially *our* fitness world.

After the boom of 2020 to 2021, digital fitness started to recalibrate, this time, against us. That massive demand during the pandemic was starting to pull back and right itself from its exponential growth. Large market swings, leaked disastrous Peloton P&Ls, and big-world events like the war in Ukraine all had their own impact on the market, investors, and consumer behavior. These massive external factors didn't just stay outside: they were starting to crush even the best, most nimble, and experienced companies. For us at CITYROW, they added fuel to the many fires burning that we were trying to extinguish, with no real luck.

So, we kept burning ourselves out despite massive pull-backs in consumer demand...but the biggest thing we were burning was cash.

The looming recession and the connected fitness hangover were descending all at once. Consumers stopped spending, and stopped spending even more so on connected fitness. Just eight months after the Series A, we had our first conversation about having to cut back: projects, staff, any extras. A board meeting followed in which I made it clear we would need to raise even more money, far sooner than we'd planned, as revenues were far below plan. The meeting was hard and yet another blow to any confidence or energy left in the tank.

How did we get here? What happened? I kept asking myself over and over again.

It was a huge, disappointing, and devastating blow to be here less than a year after the raise. I felt angry, I felt robbed. We had what it took to hit the grand slam, our programming was eons better than anything out there, we had been very early in on the digital/at-home scene, and we were one of the first fitness companies to have an omnichannel experience that was born in studios and translated into the home. It was our time to shine and we deserved to finally have our chance at bat, but that chance was slipping away.

By early 2022, we were not making our numbers—no one in the industry was—and that affected our cash burn; we were blowing through our reserves way too fast. We were trying to increase speed while the wind was fading...and we were just slowing down. We needed to increase sales on rowers, increase our subscriber base, and start to really see that post-COVID traction on the studio/franchise side...and we weren't seeing any of it.

If you look at a project as green, yellow, or red, despite the non-stop hustle from me and the team, we were all in the red. It was a combination of normal growing pains and macroeconomic factors, and many things we "could" have done differently that I've run through my head no less than 10,000 times, but no matter how hard we pushed, nothing was moving in the right direction. We were going to let our clients, team, and investors down. My head was spinning and I didn't know how we were going to be able to weather yet another storm, especially one coming at us from all directions.

Earlier on, I said that opening our first studio—after all the hype—wasn't the end, it was only the very beginning. In the same way, the Series A capital started to look like it was not the solution or the end goal, but just the beginning...or as we stood in spring 2022, maybe it was the beginning of the end.

Bottom line: I had been working for years to get to this one goal and it turns out that milestone (plus big economic factors) set the stage for a whole new set of challenges that questioned why I'd done it to begin with. It took my job as CEO so far away from CITYROW and into board rooms, investor meetings, and legal mediations.

It also made me think personally about who I was and why I've always set out to win. Thinking back to my childhood, as something of an outsider, and one who wanted to fit in—that might have positioned me to always have a chip on my shoulder, wanting to fit in, wanting to be a winner. This fuels me to put on a smiling public face even when things are crumbling in the background. And to always think about an alternative plan, a new tactic, and a way to pull another rabbit out of my hat for the win, or sometimes just to stay in the game.

Nine months after the Series A raise, we made our first round of employee cuts; we had to make another round two months later. Almost a year to the day after the zenith of the Series A, we had cut almost 75 percent of our staff, cut our burn (that is, the cash we were spending monthly), budget, and marketing, ultimately also deciding to execute a massive pivot to the company (I was down but saw one more move to make, and we were going to take it). This pivot would have us shutter our franchise operations, stop marketing digital, cut growth on tech, and partner with our manufacturer WaterRower to sell subscriptions via their existing channels. We'd plug into their existing base and grow with them, sharing upside.

In less than a year, I'd gone from building my ideal company to facing all my worst fears, and then some. We let go of the dream we'd been working on for almost a decade and transitioned into survival mode, taking one last Hail Mary shot. It was a harsh and painful transition—not to mention shocking. CITYROW was a fraction of what it looked like before, and it hit me hard. It brought me down to a place of negative self-worth, something I thought I'd long grown out of.

CHAPTER 10

TRUSTING MY CREW

As a classic human with a history of insecurities, I've been down on myself at many different times of my life. My self-worth has been challenged more times than I'd like to admit and my confidence has been rocked, shattered all the way from early elementary school to the board room. I've been physically struck down, unable to move for months post-back surgery, and I've been scarred and brought to tears by the constant No's from non-believers in the CITYROW dream.

As hard as our post-Series A downward slide was, and still is, to experience and process, nothing stung as hard as the people who let me down. Even though some people on my team stepped up in beautiful and over-the-top ways I'd never imagined, some people disappointed me deeply, people who I never thought could do that in a million years. I trusted my team to hold up their end of all aspects of execution, and while some did, some failed miserably, making me question my faith in everyone as a result, not to mention setting the company progress back meaningfully.

My leadership style is that I trust big and give a lot of latitude; I hire people I want to bet on and I let them shine. There were a ton of positive experiences with amazing people in the CITYROW trajectory. I mentioned Annie, who became the first person I hired and who'd never rowed a day in her life before I snake-charmed her into being the first member of the CITYROW crew, and whom I went all in on before we even opened our doors to become our lead instructor. I just had a gut feeling she'd make whatever needed to happen, happen. I put all my eggs in her basket, and she did the same for me. At every point, Annie was ready to tackle whatever came at her and when times got tough, she dug deep. She always rose to the occasion to teach a class even when she wasn't there mentally or to bring the energy to a last-minute TV spot. She showed up, day after day, for new challenges or the mundane day-to-day of teaching classes.

Then, there's the flip side. The ones that I trusted big and who let me and the company down in monumental ways. I had senior executives who I trusted whole-heartedly cause irreparable damage to the business. One of the most important people in the business quit one day with *zero* notice. Another senior executive who had a whole arm of the business in their control completely botched multiple projects at the most critical time. There were HR nightmares. Employees made questionable decisions. A few early employees were given too much latitude and then had to be firmly reeled (yanked?!) in. I trusted people, big time, and unfortunately that led to too much blind trust. I believed in people, I bet on them: but some of those people just didn't show up for shifts, multiple times over. They said and confirmed one thing but it never happened. The mistakes and people failures almost crippled the company.

I thought it was the right thing to give people the freedom to let them fly and instead that was what prevented me from seeing failures until it was almost too late.

A few of the younger women I hired taught me an important lesson: While my friends in my personal life are everything to me, friends in business are a very gray area. I trusted (and cared about) my employees and team members, but I had to establish boundaries. When the company was celebrating something or when they wanted to go out drinking together, there came a time that I always had to start cutting out early (after learning this lesson the hard way) or declining invites to their parties, events, or entering conversations that cross a personal line. It's truly a judgment call in the moment, but that kind of thing often feels too far for business. It's great to get to know people but I probably shouldn't be the person you seek relationship advice from, you know? That realization was especially hard, but an important discovery for me. I love being *that* person and friend, and I think I'm pretty good at it, but after a few years, I learned how important those boundaries are in business. Sadly, I'm first their boss, then their friend, and that's the order I need to make decisions within. Establishing that distinction was an important one for any growing leader, especially for me, as someone who always wanted to make friends (and even more so when I had such a hard time doing it in my early life).

It was a fine line between building a culture of camaraderie and teamwork with likeminded people who had fun at work (while building epic things) and setting up the right policies and boundaries (both personal and related to HR) to ensure it was making it clear that this was a mature company—not a sorority or social club.

Is there such a thing as too much faith in people in business, and in life? Maybe. But ultimately, for the real people problems I encountered, and the general challenges in leading a company, some that I'll likely relive over and over in my head for years to come like a bad sitcom rerun, I blamed myself. I know there was no controlling the pandemic or the consumer pull-back that followed, but for our people—that I had full purview over—I'll always beat myself up for things I didn't catch. I felt like I should have seen more earlier, I should have had a tighter grasp, but I'm (unfortunately) only human and couldn't do it all, didn't see it all. At the time, I couldn't be everywhere and also lead in a way that felt authentic to me.

(In retrospect, this was and is unhealthy negative self-talk. Today I remind myself that I did the very best I could—all my self-blame was just insecurity—and not many male founders would ever blame themselves in the same way.)

Part of my leadership style and the ethos CITYROW was built on is "high autonomy and high expectations." With every partner I have, then and now, it's how I operate. I trust big and I expect equal amounts of dedication and work product. Some may say those expectations are too high but when I think about the importance of what I'm trusting people with, you can't set expectations high enough.

My favorite quote is an African proverb: "If you want to go fast, go alone, if you want to go far, go together." I always knew I wanted to go far, so that meant I had to let people into CITYROW, trust them, and risk them letting me down. I hire slowly, bet on people, and once I trust, I trust completely. I take your word. I don't micromanage. I don't think you should "triple check" that—just go for it. I don't need to read that email. Just send it. You got this, right? And I know that a lot of people who have worked with me historically love that type of leadership style and thrive on the fact that I trust them completely. I know that I've built up people's confidence, not to mention their dedication to the company, and that contributes more to company success than the extra sentence or an edit I might have added to their email. I've built up their ability to grow. I'm only paying it forward, by the way. In the early days of my career, I was trusted in many cases in areas I probably shouldn't have been! But that's what allowed me to grow and build my confidence. And so, I'll bet on people all day long.

What I expect in return is that they're going to deliver, to *over*deliver, because those are the types of people that I surround myself with, particularly in CITYROW.

And in a young company, there's a lot to do. There are endless things to do. So, if there's someone on the team who says, *I got this*, then I'm going to trust you that indeed you got that.

What I learned is that I need to take more than their word to make sure they actually got it—layer in the right levels of checks and balances that are authentic with high levels of trust. At the same time, I should also protect the downside, which ended up happening on the tech side of the business and on the operations side. And that downside happened with a lot of our advisors, too.

From the very early days, I collected peripheral advisors like trophies, amazing people that wanted to be part of what we were building. Everyone in life needs advisors and mentors, especially when you're young and don't have "bosses," per se. While I was technically the boss/CEO/chair of the board, I was self-aware enough to know I was also in my late twenties and early thirties, and there was much to be learned from those who came before me. As a self-proclaimed lifelong learner, I had to cultivate a stable of people to learn from on my own, and I was very enthusiastic any time I met someone that could be remotely helpful—to me and/

or CITYROW—and/or whose name, credibility, experience and network could help us grow.

In the early days of the business, I didn't know how to be vulnerable and ask for help. Like a brave face and "I got this," it was almost a chronic problem with me. I didn't know where to turn and who to trust outside of my core set of people like my friends Dan or Jeff.

Then I started expanding my trust forcefield a little bit, dipping a toe in the waters outside that tight circle. By the time of the Series A, we were buzzing in the world of tech and connected fitness, and more people were interested in working with us, too.

But before the Series A and the influx, the investor and eventual CITYROW board member Arie was the one who really taught me that there was meaningful value in bringing in the right people alongside me as investors and even board members.

I was at first extremely resistant to letting people in, a direct result of my sometimes hidden but always there somewhere control-freak side (yes, I'm the eldest sibling and a female). I'd heard a lot of horror stories about boards, everything from their ability to seize control and oust the CEO, to doing a full takeover. While those things felt far away and would never happen to CITYROW, I tried to make sure it wasn't on the table for as long as possible. Plus, I always thought I'd be a better dictator than a governor, so I never really imagined having a board at all before the Series A.

The other side of me, though, was feeling to my core the "it's lonely at the top" aphorism. I was hungry for guidance, and for people to stand shoulder to shoulder with me as we faced the next battles, ideally, people who'd been through some of these battles before. There was no way I should (or wanted to) face this all alone.

Arie had the right energy, the right demeanor, and the right experience to teach me that the right people around you co-governing can be a game-changer. That opened my eyes a little bit to letting more people in to help. Not only was that so important for the company, but for me as a growing leader and executive, too.

He brought some cool people to the table, and told me, "If you like them, maybe make them an official advisor."

Previously, all CITYROW equity was really reserved for employees. But then I started understanding that I had a little bit to play with and could maybe sprinkle it to drive the business forward, and also reward those who'd gone above and beyond when there was nowhere left to turn and when the risk was far greater (remember Mike, the contractor/investor/advisor? People like him). These were people who had been around before, whom I always knew were only a phone call away. And then, suddenly, I had the ability to thank them and reward them.

After we raised the Series A, I also saw the opportunity to give some equity to the right high-caliber people as advisors to drive growth. We now had the cache to attract a different level of advisors and talent to learn from and help further the brand.

I was so excited about finally working with a couple of people I had looked up to for years. Worshiped, in fact. I couldn't believe I was starting an actual business relationship with them. Holy fuck.

They would say things like, "To be an advisor, I want X, Y, and, oh yeah, Z amount of equity."

And I replied immediately, "Okay, amazing, yes, we can definitely make that work."

We got this. We have some money in the bank. These people are going to represent the brand, post about us, and really help us *here, here,* and *here.* We customized scopes of work for them based on the right lanes of each advisor's skill set. I was thrilled.

I think I was a *little* too enamored, and looked to these big names as a stamp of approval—for me, for CITYROW, for everything we were doing and everything we had built—rather than really sitting down and figuring out how we were going to truly take advantage of every single hour that they were going to give us. No, that they were *charging* us for in some way or another.

I wish I'd thought that through more instead of acting so quickly to say, "Yes!! Join us!" I wish I'd mapped out much more thoroughly their roles and responsibilities. And I wish I'd let them come to us a little bit more, telling us directly how they could help us and what we should be doing in a bunch of different ways, instead of me jumping all over them like a puppy (at least in my head). So, I learned a lot of lessons there. (And now that the tides have turned and I face the opportunity of being that advisor to other growing companies and founders, I try to impart that lesson. Pay it forward, remember?)

As for my CITYROW advisors, I trusted them…and didn't realize how much I was going to have to *manage* them. As a result, many let me down.

From my very first internship, I was great at managing down, but the magic skill set I'd mastered was also managing up. That's a killer thing to master, and it's about anticipating and understanding people's needs. I'm fortunate that this came naturally to me and was certainly a factor in my early success at work. When I was working at Condé Nast, my boss was in Europe on the day an important monthly report came out. I remember not even thinking twice—it was a weird, long deck PDF and I translated it into a quick email for her that contained the exact things that I knew she would want to know coming out of that report. I sent it to her within ten minutes of the report coming out.

"How did you know I wanted this?" she asked me incredulously over Messenger.

I can always sense what other people are going to want or need, and so managing up comes as naturally to me as managing more junior people.

There were a few investors, advisors, and board members I had to learn how to navigate from the Series A on, though, where that didn't happen quite as naturally... or at all.

4/10/23 CITYROW INVESTOR UPDATE

... As you might remember from our last update, it was critical to exit the high-cost direct-to-consumer sales market and pivot into a hardware and content distribution model with our long-term partner, WaterRower.

Progress so far has been slow and a struggle. All manufacturers in our sector are seeing sales slow significantly given the post-COVID headwinds and the challenging macroeconomic environment significantly reducing home fitness equipment sales. For City-Row, this means retailers are taking on less inventory and our content/app is exposed to a much smaller pool of new customers

... we missed our targets by a wide margin....we're doing more work to add new marketing layers... starting to see some improvement, but not enough to make up for the last few months... we are creatively executing... reduced costs further... made deeper cuts to the team... we are getting creative with

bringing in new revenue by renting out our production space and providing additional services to WaterRower… we only hit 35 percent of target so must find another path forward if there is one…

While we are still very much in the midst of this connected fitness hangover, I still strongly believe, and the long-term signs continue to point to, the fact that digital/connected is here to stay, but first, we must weather this perfect storm.

For those not familiar with the market happenings, included are links to articles for additional context:

> *Lululemon "Pivots Away" From Mirror*
> *Athlete Investors Can't Save Tonal's Falling $500 Million Valuation*
> *More Rough Waters for Rowing Startup Hydrow*

Due to this challenging industry environment, we are accelerated M&A activity.

As always, I will keep you apprised of our progress.

Best,

Helaine

❧

Trust is two ways, I've learned. Huge for me to learn. One of the many corollary lessons I've learned is that I need to ask for help but also be transparent, which is always hard for anyone when you're delivering bad news but hit me extra hard given my history as an outsider—I didn't want people to think less of me. When things weren't going well after the Series A, I paused before asking for help from my board, the people who were paid to be there to do just that, because I was so far in the weeds. Hindsight always makes everything so much clearer.

Instead, my "I got this" energy bubbled up again, breaking the surface. *I got this, I can solve it.* I never had a board before and I didn't quite grasp that part of their job is to sweep in when the company is navigating rough waters.

That made me realize that I'm not perfect—not even close—and that I'm still not great at trusting people. I'm afraid of letting everyone down.

I also realized something huge, which is that I dipped back into my feeling of being an outsider long ago the whole time we were striving for the Series A. I spent seven years wanting to be a part of the inner circle of tech—the *TechCrunch* crew of venture-backed businesses.

And then once we got in, I just wanted to get out. It turns out that my authentic self doesn't necessarily actually want to be a part of that (mostly bro) club. I'm a creative who wants to forge my own unique path.

CITYROW was its own beast; in fact, at best, according to legacy investor thinking, half of it should have been ven-ture-backed and half of it should not have been backed by multi-unit brick-and-mortar investors. The two sides of the business had two entirely different economic structures. But that's not how a founder thinks—to me, the future needed these combined, and that's what a creative thinker does. Founders don't create based on how things were done in the

past, or on tradition, but innovates and dreams on what the world needs tomorrow.

Unfortunately, that meant I created a mutt... an un-fundable mutt.

As I mentioned before, I wish I'd leaned more on our board and investors earlier with our challenges, looping them into being part of the solution. I was trying to do it all alone, when I had a group of people ready to help. The board, once they learned that momentum was slowing while cash burn continued, contributing to our dire financial straits, stepped in to problem-solve alongside me. Again, that two-way street (or maybe intersection) of trust.

And so, what happens then when I trust big and expect big things is that the disappointment hits bigger. It's because I trusted so deeply and probably with pieces of my heart that I shouldn't even bring into business in the first place.

When natural things occur, like when people leave, or the company faces challenges, I find myself getting hurt on top of the business side of things. That's just me. I think there's a lot of power in vulnerability, which comes with the leadership style that I've chosen, as deeply difficult as it makes things for me, versus less obviously "feeling" (that is, emotional) founders.

I can only show up as a leader in the way I am in the world and for me, and that meant navigating relationships in the best way I could—trusting big, showing up big, and sometimes not always getting it right. All the while realizing that I'm a person under the founder, under the CEO in the boardroom, not a robot, and will feel things that pierce my armor. But I'll still show up as long as I can, with my brave face, in the center of the arena, ready to keep fighting until there's truly nothing left to fight for.

CHAPTER 11

BAILING OUT THE WATER BEFORE WE SINK

A DAY IN THE LIFE OF HELAINE KNAPP, POWERHOUSE FOUNDER, AND CEO OF CITYROW, SPRING 2022

6:00 a.m.: Alarm—which is ironically "Firework" by Katy Perry—blasts through my consciousness, waking me out of a sound sleep. Got about five hours in, when I really need a solid nine most nights. I think I had a couple nightmares but could also be parts of my real life seeping into my dreams. Remind myself to mention this in my next therapy appointment.

6:09 a.m.: Think about meditating. Dismiss that thought almost immediately and instead I hit snooze.

6:18 a.m.: Hit snooze again. Have guilt about hitting said snooze. Remind myself to go to bed earlier. Do a one-eyed Wordle to try and wake my brain up.

6:26 a.m.: Katy Perry again. Gotta get my ass up or I'll regret it. Skim through emails from bed despite knowing this is not part of an ideal morning routine.

6:40 a.m.: Shit, where did the past forty minutes go? Reluctantly peel myself out of bed and head to the kitchen, pouring a massive glass of iced coffee and forcing myself to chew through a banana.

6:51 a.m.: In the car, trying not to speed, and hoping to make it to my tennis game on time. For this, I should have left ten minutes earlier so I have time to tie my shoes and fill up my water bottle, but what can you do?

7:05 a.m.: I turn off my smartwatch to avoid seeing any messages that would inevitably throw me off my game (literally and figuratively), and start to play. I relax a couple millimeters and have a great game. I thank myself for the banana. I'm smiling by the end…until I turn my watch back on and see that it's 8:30 a.m. already and I need to be on a call with my board by 9 a.m. Fuck. I shout my goodbyes and sprint to the parking lot.

8:37 a.m.: I'm sitting in traffic, sweating, not because of tennis, but because I cannot be late for this call.

8:49 a.m.: Miraculously, I made it home and I now have eleven minutes to shower and blow dry the sweat out of my hair. I throw on a professional button down with a fresh pair of leggings. You can take the girl out of COVID, but some habits die hard.

9:00 a.m.: Ignoring my desire for another cup of coffee and a monster smoothie, I clear my throat, paste on a smile, and with a cheery "Good morning, crew!" let the board members into the meeting from the waiting room.

9:07 a.m.: The board meeting implodes. Ignoring my greeting, the board chair informs me unceremoniously that we needed to make even deeper—the deepest I'd ever imagined—cuts to our company budget. This comes a measly ten days after the previous round of cuts, where I had to fire my colleagues (and friends). I'm still not over one of the toughest discussions from that day. I had actually—and obviously accidentally—put the script for the conversation *in the calendar invite* for one of the employees I was letting go, so they could see in advance what was going to happen.

In that meeting, I was sobbing so hard I couldn't even get the words out, and my cofounder Ashley had to take over. Remembering this distracts me from the business at hand, and I force myself away from the pity party and back into the shit show.

9:27 a.m.: Despite my preparation in the days leading up to this board meeting, even the knowledge in the back of my mind that more cuts like this might happen, it's still a stark reminder to me that everything around me was falling apart to at least some degree. The board and the investors were incredibly hard to manage because we didn't seem to have a mutual understanding; I felt like a failure. It really was a living nightmare.

9:33 a.m.: I have to go off camera to get a tissue because I'm overwhelmed, stressed, still emotional from the past few weeks, and unable to hold back the tears. A powerful badass CEO is not supposed to cry. This thought compounds, making me feel worse, like the tears make me more of a loser—and I cry that much harder.

9:45 a.m.: The board call ends. My follow-up work is a beast. I have to re-cast another model, creating three potential scenarios for how we can move forward as a company and a detailed update on our new strategy, along with projections with input from our new investment partner (which I have no idea how I'm going to get). But I commit to it all by the end of the week because I know that's what I have to do to instill confidence in me in the board. It's a funny thing to be determined to instill confidence when you're still crying from the overwhelming stress.

9:46 a.m.: I now have fourteen minutes until I have to be on camera again, this time for a live segment about post-pandemic business trends on *Cheddar* TV.

9:47 a.m.: I lay down on the couch with ice cubes on my eyes, hoping that sixty seconds will magically eliminate the redness and puffiness.

9:48 a.m.: I jump up, put on some bronzer, reapply mascara, pinch my cheeks, and apply a copious amount of dry shampoo and texturizing spray into my hair to make it seem like I wasn't on the tennis court a mere ninety minutes ago. Men really have it easy when it comes to hair. I look in the mirror practicing the smile and calm demeanor I in no way feel.

10:05 a.m.: I get through the three-minute *Cheddar* segment with—miracle #2—flying colors. "Can you come back again next week?" the producer asked me when I finished up. *I'm thirsty, I'm hungry, and I need to sit down,* is all I could think by way of a response. Standing desks, for all their glory, are not what I need right now. I have six minutes to satiate all my needs.

10:11 a.m.: I pace around my apartment, psyching myself up for the 10:15 a.m. CITYROW all-hands team meeting. My phone buzzes in my hand. "MOM" blares across the screen. I decline the call. She calls again, probably thinking she dialed wrong. I turn my phone on silent.

10:15 a.m.: The meeting starts. The vibe is solemn, even over Zoom. After all, it's our first meeting since we had to lay off 75 percent of the staff the week before. Thankfully Ashley built a beautiful up-beat but also factual deck. But no matter what was going on, it was my job to show up for the (remaining) team. We have to keep moving forward, somehow, some way. I'd been up for less than four hours but felt the desperate need for a nap. Regardless, I pour everything I have into it, and I hope they feel it too. As a leader, and especially in times of crisis, you need to bring even more to a video call to make up for the virtual nature of it. By the time we've gone through updates, I'm completely depleted. And my day has barely even started.

11:00 a.m.–1:53 p.m.: I can't quite tell you what I did. Emails. Rain-making. Negotiating. Placating. Then I look at my calendar and realize two things: aside from my banana at dawn, I hadn't eaten enough today and I have an investor pitch at 2 p.m. I quickly scarf a few bites of leftover salad and some slightly stale pretzels as I glance through the materials about the VC firm I am about to meet with. The Diet Coke saved for emergencies (a.k.a., daily) artificially brings me back to life.

1:59 p.m.: I close my eyes, take a deep breath, and muster all the confidence I can from my depleted stores. I am really scraping the bottom of the barrel, and coming up pretty short. I glance down at my phone (which I had turned back on) and see forty-seven new texts on the group chat with my high school friends. Either someone is having a baby or someone has a flat tire and is workshopping solutions with the group. I want to but can't get into that now, so I re-silence my phone.

2:00 p.m.: Why am I talking now to new investors? Good question. Along with having to let most of my team go, I also recently had our top investor back out of a multimillion-dollar bridge round of funding, and once again, I needed to keep the ship afloat. Also, for months I had been talking to a venture group that was not just going to be badass investors in the fitness and wellness space, but some of the major players were women. I got connected to them through one of our advisors, and for the first time in my fundraising, it felt like it was coming together and all made sense. I took so many calls with them, and we got really far along in the process. I thought it was a Yes, with a solid $250,000 or $500,000 to start, with lots of room to grow. That would have really kickstarted everything, giving us momentum for more. Instead, they dicked me around for months and months. The main guy I was dealing with, as it turned out, was a classic VC asshole that doesn't get back to you. In our final call, I thought that I was going to be talking to a decision-maker but it was a junior associate who was clearly texting the whole time and hardly heard a word I said. It was a big blow. So, for this meeting, I manage to bring my passion to the table, but being freshly discouraged from my most recent experience, I'm not sure it was enough. Well, I *know* it wasn't enough because he declined to invest "at this challenging time."

The next couple of hours pass in another blur, and suddenly, it's 5:00 p.m.

5:25 p.m.: I stare into my closet, though instead of focusing on what I'm going to wear to the dinner I have to go to that night with some of my investors/board members, I go through every conceivable excuse to not go I can think of—my cat died (I don't actually have one, I hate cats), food poisoning (too obvious), newly-diagnosed chronic fatigue syndrome (feels like it, but no), a flash flood (not out of the question in Miami but not forecasted for that particular night).

7:10 p.m.: I step out of the Uber, dread in my gut and a big smile on my face. "There she is!" I hear someone bellow as I walk into the restaurant. I turn and walk toward the table where my group is—all men, all white, all with martinis in front of them (and by the looks of some of them, not their first)—and sit down, steeling myself. One of them pours me a huge glass of wine from the bottle chilling off to the side, interrupting my feeble "I wasn't going to drink ton–" with a wave of his hand.

9:10 p.m.: Entrees have finally been finished (*How can it possibly take so long to eat some grilled fish and steak?* I wonder), and I can see my end in sight. I start to plot my escape. I've been talking about my tennis match in the morning to set the stage for me not being able to stay out too late. Someone waves to the server in the universal hand signal for another round. Shit.

10:25 p.m.: We've moved onto shots and there is discussion of the next lounge and then a late-night strip club. After the loudest "Cheers!" yet, shot glasses clink, and as they're gulping, I dump my tequila shot out to the side of my lap (I haven't been able to drink tequila since college and tonight's not the time to try again), praying it doesn't splash the woman at the table behind me.

10:41 p.m.: I finally, *finally* manage to make my excuses, extricate myself, and get in the Uber, staring out at the lights as we speed up the causeway. I fall into bed, knowing this day is going to

rinse and repeat, a warped, millennial Groundhog
Day with no end in sight.

❧

It wasn't just keeping up the strength internally with our team and
inner circle; for close to a decade, I had to project a smiling face,
write punchy and upbeat LinkedIn posts, and sit as the sparkly and
wise guest on podcast after podcast. The need to keep up a public
face even when I was in the throes of the lows, after I'd just spent
the previous thirty minutes sobbing or getting told a firm No from
someone who never gave me the time of day, and ultimately finding and keeping faith in myself despite the shit storm life throws at
me, was simply a skill I had to master... and I did, quickly.

The thing I had not mastered yet was the answer to the question, *Where is the space for me to deal with all of it?*

The hits that hit CITYROW (and me as the first line of defense)
rattled my core and my shaky foundation of confidence—it took
me back to the early days of my life when I was building confidence
and a sense of self and often made me question that confidence and
self worth over and over again.

Yes, I'm a total badass. But on the inside, I'm that shy kid who
had no friends at camp. I'm deeply sensitive (I've always worried
I'm too sensitive to even be a CEO/leader) and while I thought
the pandemic and the multi-year buildup to the Series A was hard
and pushed me past my limits, that was nothing compared to what
I was dealing with in the year that followed.

I had to lay off my friends, tell my co-founders we were not getting paid, close studios, comfort franchisees, and re-configure the
entire business strategy. And then somehow show up for everyone

else, often minutes apart from being hit with another disaster, and be the strength and visionary for our employees, investors, and clients.

Also, I was in deep burn-out so I felt every hit even harder; my armor was whittling away after ten years of taking hits.

Burnout is a raw and real feeling. While I thought I'd experienced burnout at times over the years, I never fully felt it until that year following our Series A raise. Running on empty means there's nothing left to weather blows, and that's part of why I kept crying in places I probably shouldn't have. I had reached my limit of defensive lines and was cracked open.

My brand of burnout looks like grief (which is probably part of the process I'm going through as the company completely changes course in the hopes of some sort of positive outcome or exit) and everyday tears. I've eroded down to the bone, where there are no walls left to keep up the external facade.

It was probably through these conversations that I started to process what was going on. While I was in the middle of obliterating two-thirds of my business baby and firing everyone, I also had to personally deal with the fact and confront the reality that this business that I'd dedicated a decade of my life to, that my friends gave their heart and souls to, and that my friends, family, and close confidants put hard cash behind, might not turn into the dream we'd been striving toward. That tidal wave of sadness, disappointment, fear, and harsh reality crashed into me time and time again during this time and for many months after.

One positive that came out is that I learned (well, I was basically forced to) to lean on people, let go, and let it be. Luckily, I have a support system and rotated calling people in tears when I needed that pep talk/pick-me-up. I still kind of hate asking for this support when I need it most, but I needed and still need support.

My village always shows up to remind me who I was, who I am, and what I'm capable of. Whereas I as the artist see mostly tarnish, pain, and areas of improvement, those a step removed see with awe the strength, grit, innovation, and determination. Despite the harsh self-criticism, I would not be defined by the series of events in this current shit show.

CHAPTER 12

IT ALL COMES DOWN TO ME

My village shows up, and my tribe has always been—and will always be—my *thing*. Even in the worst of times, I've been lucky (and maybe smart) enough to surround myself with the best of people.

The people should always be the first, biggest, and most important element of a company, and they were that and more in the CITYROW story.

As an individual, a leader, a founder, and a CEO, though, you can have the greatest of the great alongside you, but at the end of the day, it still all comes down to you. So, while I had *the* crew, the best people alongside and with me, it still all came down to me. That meant tactically that no matter how hard or complex a problem, no matter how much I didn't think I was qualified to lead us to the solution, I had to. As the founder, CEO, leader, there's no delegation for the biggest problems, only partners to help solve them. You can never tap out, you must always tap in.

"It all comes down to me" also means it's up to me to deal with the highs and lows of the emotional journey, knowing it's "nothing personal," all the while building confidence, trust in myself, and then looking forward and looking out for myself, because truly no one else will. This is a journey of betting on yourself in every way that matters and never taking your eyes off the road.

"It all comes down to me" is tactical.

There's no outsourcing. You cannot delegate the big stuff. The little stuff you can—and should—delegate all day long, but the big stuff, the good alongside the bad, is all you. That means I navigated the crazy lawsuits and I was featured on the *Today* show.

I have to figure out the creative solutions, pull rabbits out of my hat; the spotlight shines on me, I get the mic and have to have the answer when everyone else doesn't know what to do. I can call in assistance, recruits, lawyers, support, a team to brainstorm the best path, but I am responsible. I must step up to the plate and be ready for what's around the corner, because there is no one else who's in this as deep and would take a fastball to the face for this company. I might not feel like I'm always ready, but tapping out has worse consequences. It was impossibly hard at times, but I did not and cannot shy away from responsibility and accountability. Even if my insecurities make it seem like there's someone better suited for something, I might collaborate, but I can't ever pass it off 100 percent.

It also means tactically that you're responsible when your team needs you to be. It was 2016 and we were doing an epic CITYROW pop-up on Under Armour's rooftop at the famous

Starrett-Lehigh building in NYC. This was a *huge* activation for us and we'd dragged twenty rowers up to their rooftop patio where we'd be doing live classes all weekend with a backdrop of the NYC skyline. It was a hot ticket in town and one of our most prestigious "gets" to date. With a tiny team, it was all hands on deck and myself, Ashley and two other members of our team showed up in our matching CITYROW gear at 7:15 a.m. on a Saturday to meet the Under Armour rep and set up before classes started at 8:30 a.m.

We arrived at the office entrance and it was locked—our partner wasn't there yet. We called, texted, called again, and eventually went to the front desk to try and gain access. We were locked out and had no idea where our partner was to open the door so we could set up. By 8 a.m., we started to panic, because we already didn't have enough time and now we *really* didn't. The front desk was pretending like this was Fort Knox and we couldn't get anyone on the phone from our Under Armour partner. It was high stress.

As we sat feeling like lost puppies outside the office with all of our supplies for the event piled up around us, Ashley turned to me and said plainly, "Go downstairs and don't come back without a key." She put this on me and told me to go solve this issue, and she was right.

I went downstairs and talked Bruce, the front desk manager, into letting us into the space.

At 8:45 a.m. our rep arrived, with messy hair and blurry eyes (she had clearly gone a little too hard the night before!). She was extremely apologetic and horrified that she'd overslept. Little did she realize that we were a few minutes away from a total disaster and I was forced to, once again, go above and beyond to push and push and push to save the day.

Stories like this are weekly occurrences in the day to day start-up life. You can rely on people, partners and vendors, but more often than not, you need to rely on yourself and your skillsets to ensure success.

"It all comes down to me" is the ability to weather those emotional highs and lows.

In a start-up, the highs of highs and the lows of lows are extreme—a major press release alongside a lawsuit, often at the same time, within hours of each other, and it's up to you to navigate them, not getting too caught up in the extremities, but to keep the balance. It's funny because, in reality, some of the highs and the lows would likely not be that meaningful if you were a big corporation. A great bit of press, a good quarter, a frivolous lawsuit. They're common at that point, they don't sway such a big ship. But in a small start-up vessel, the waves hit you more violently, and the peaks in between are really, really, really steep. They will likely get a little calmer as the company matures and the boat grows but it's a long time before they even out.

As a founder, you're the captain. It's up to you to personally ride every peak and every valley. You surf the big and small waves, and sometimes you fall off, crumble, and cry, but you must get back up because another wave is coming and that's what you signed up for. There's no one out there to tow you back in and you can't just bob on your board forever.

So, it comes down to me to be even-keeled, and able to ride the start-up roller coaster, knowing it's part of the journey—it's nothing different from the reality you have to face as a human being going through this life. Developing resilience is the antidote. It's what helps you weather any and all storms no matter what kind of waves (or tsunamis) come your way in every single part of life.

"It all comes down to me" means nothing is personal.

It all comes down to me...but it's not all *about* me.

You know by now I'm a very sensitive person, which may (or may not) sometimes work against me in business. I take everything to heart, especially every interaction I have with people in my purview, mainly because I care so much.

But here's a very big secret I've learned that has changed my life (and many others when this resonates): Almost nothing is personal. Every single person out there is dealing with their own pile of crap on a day-to-day basis, and that might spill over into their interactions with me, especially if those interactions are less than positive.

Take spring 2022 when the markets were imploding and I was trying to raise that round of follow-up capital. Some conversations with stakeholders turned nasty, people were prickly, some went on tangents that were mean...and those had nothing to do with me or CITYROW. The reality was they were also all dealing with a lot of stressors, and if I put myself in their shoes, I'd see that most of their portfolio companies were hitting breaking points and valuations were slashed and millions to billions of dollars were lost. That's why they were prickly. If they put on their rational hat with zero emotion, they'd all get that but that's not how humans work, that's not how life works. Everyone brings their own baggage to every conversation and business is no different (even if we think it should be).

It's always hard when a board member sends me an aggressive text, or someone inadvertently makes a comment that makes me feel "less than."

But I've taught myself to step outside those kinds of situations and see them for what they really are—and what they are is not about me, but the other person and about business. I'm just the representative receiving the information. And then that becomes about me managing how I react to what's happening in the business, and outside of it, too. This isn't middle school, this isn't about hurt feelings. This is business, and I've needed to remember and remind myself of this over and over. Probably for the rest of my life. I can't control someone else's behavior or actions, but I can choose my own emotions and how I react. I can work on what gets me off balance and what I can weather, getting stronger over the years. As with most muscles, I've grown to be able to let much more roll off—some waves seem like nothing these days—but I can also appreciate that it hasn't always been the case and I had to go through those early storms to be where I am today.

"It all comes down to me" means trusting myself.

We all have to keep learning the same lessons over and over again, especially me. Trusting (myself) is a big one. In childhood, I had to learn to rely on myself. In my early adulthood, I had to slowly start trusting myself. And in later years, I've had to become incredibly self-aware in order to keep going and being resilient. Then, I bet on myself. Confidence, self-worth, resilience—the lessons keep showing up, just in different ways.

Trusting myself is about using that self-awareness muscle I've built up over my years of open enrollment in the school of hard knocks.

"It all comes down to me" means looking out for myself.

As entwined as CITYROW and I have been, I've learned more recently that it's important for me to figure out my identity outside the company. Some of that means figuring out what's next, not just for the company but also for me—even/especially when it's entirely uncertain—and some of that is separating myself from all of it entirely. It's as simple as reminding myself that I am not CITYROW and CITYROW is not me; CITYROW is a beautiful thing I built alongside amazing people but I am not the company. As founder, even just hearing and repeating that is important.

There's something terrifying and exciting about (re)engineering new goals in this new, quieter, simpler world that's coming down the pike for me. Potentially in a world when I'm not running CITYROW.

There's a lot of self-talk here. It all comes down to me, but it's not about me; it's not personal, don't take anything personally; the only thing you can control is you and you must look out for yourself. This start-up thing is challenging; it's beautiful, but it's hard, not just in the doing and in the executing, but being in it as a human. As a human being with feelings, it's hard to truly not take something personally, no matter how rationally we know that to be true and no matter how much we separate ourselves from the business.

The difficulty also comes tactically when I'm burned out and tired and really and truly don't know what to do next. I want to hand the keys over to someone else to take it through the next phase, wanting so badly to sit this play out and let someone else who has done it before have the at-bat solo. In the last few innings, the projects and stakes are bigger. While I might not be the most seasoned at the specific task at hand, and while I know I'm not the company, I am its best player and captain and I would never take myself out of any big plays.

CHAPTER 13

LANDING THE PLANE

The last chapter of the story cuts deep.

You must always have the goal, the Big Hairy Audacious Goal, but at some point, you must also have two feet on the ground and realize that maybe the circumstances aren't going to allow that right now.[1]

No matter how great I know our brand, product, and team are, no one is safe from the biggest waves, and we got tossed around just like everyone else. I'm here to put us back together in the best way I know how and then find the right closing chapter, even if it's far from the "rainbows and butterfly" dream I envisioned for so long.

We had embarked a year prior on our Hail Mary pass—a distribution deal with our manufacturer in which we'd pause expensive consumer marketing and build out an acquisition channel through

---

[1]   Collins, Jim, *Good to Great*, Harper, New York 2001.

their existing sales channels and existing clients. We'd essentially partner with the manufacturer, share in the upside, and sell the CITYROW app to people that already owned rowers, and the app alongside new rower sales.

So what that looked like in practice is that we would downscale our internal operations and put a tactical plan in place alongside our manufacturing partner. We learned their system and their sales channels and used our marketing prowess on their audience. Rather than spend into the digital ether, grasping for new clients that could come from anywhere, we focused on the one niche we knew loved us and likely already had a rower—this way we were shifting from selling rowers to just selling our app as an add-on, which was a much easier sell for $29 a month versus almost $2,000 in rower hardware!

It was a really good move that was a win-win for us and our manufacturer who was always looking for more ways to engage and delight their customers. We would send emails to their base to, "Get more out of your WaterRower!" and would include physical inserts with a QR code to download the app with every new purchase. We also worked with them to sell our CITYROW machine on their retailers floors nationwide. Within three months we were in over a hundred stores and had a fleet of people selling the machine. They were happy to have a new piece of equipment and we were happy to have teams working the sale in person. They'd get the revenue from the rower and we'd get the subscription dollars, the most valuable part to our business.

On paper it looked great and all parties were eager to get moving. Our team and investors and board loved the plan as it reduced our operational burn and set a path to profitability if a fraction of projections were hit.

It was a great plan in concept, but it failed out the gate, and we had a short window to deliver. A fraction of projections were not it.

The industry continued to spiral downward and the sluggish sales were affecting all areas of fitness, and finally affecting our manufacturer to whom we'd hitched our wagon for this final play.

All parties gave it everything, but ultimately the timing of the partnership launch, coupled with a lot of new infrastructure needs to support these new initiatives, led to a very slow ramp up period. Would this work if we had two to three years to see results? I feel 100 percent that yes it would've worked. But it didn't—we had to move too fast and had too short of a window to drive results before our runway ran out.

At that point, then, it was clear that it was time for us to prepare for the end and see how we could reach it in the best way possible. Truth be told, I'd been mentally preparing for this to be an outcome for the year prior and given the tumultuous past twelve-plus months, not to mention eight-plus years. While I still looked for long term opportunities to invest and grow, they were not materializing. I knew we'd fought every battle to date until the final breath and we'd give this final initiative every drop we had left in the tank. During this time I cried most days. Between calls, as I fell asleep, during a walk. I was devastated and after years of holding it together for everyone else, I started to crumble. The weight of the past ten years—the hope, the dreams, the plans—I cried big tears for it all. For months.

One weekend I was hosting friends at a beach rental and a few hours into their visit I just broke. I couldn't entertain, I couldn't be normal, I was lost and needed space. Even from some of my favorite people in the world, but I was in deep. I ended up leaving my own house and driving to Annie's house nearby, able to express the devastation and commiserate together was all I could do... and watch old movies and eat popcorn.

It was the first time ever in our ten years that I did not have a vision for CITYROW as a stand-alone company on our path forward. It was a new and scary place to be. At each and every challenging juncture prior, Ashley or I could see clearly what we needed to do for the future success of the business, often getting frustrated when others couldn't see with the clarity that one of us had. However, the industry we were in had changed so much as a result of COVID and the pandemic that from where we stood, there was no path forward.

I was coming to terms with the feeling, and the meaning. Just like anyone who deals with deep sadness and loss, it overcame me with emotion and the tears came often.

During this time I sought advice from board members, mentors and advisors on exploring every possible angle forward for the business. A year prior we'd been at a crossroads and through this type of discovery and outreach we'd found a path forward—the one I described above with our manufacturer. Now, I was back to the drawing board after a failed hail-mary pass to see if there were any more paths forward. Were there any plays left to try? If there were, I'd find them.

I reached deep into the CITYROW bench to speak to each and every person who surrounded this business; I updated them on where the business was, how the partnership was going (or not going) and where the overall industry was (shattered). I had my AirPods in while walking and talking for months. My step count skyrocketed, but during all those hours of calls and brainstorms, nothing cracked open except for me as I slowly let everyone in on not just helping me solve the problems, but also when they asked how I was doing, I didn't sugar coat it. "I'm not awesome, I'll be ok but this is taking a toll on me."

The market, which had been "frothy" just a year prior, was now very tight, so new money was hard to come by, and customer acquisition costs—how we'd get new customers by way of marketing and advertising —was astronomically high. We'd tried the partnership route.

The only remaining option that seemed viable was a deeper partnership—to try to hit a home run with an M&A (Mergers and Acquisition) process.

As hard as it was to swallow, no matter how hard I'd fought, there was no strong path forward outside of a big partnership like an M&A. The diligence I did during this time helped me channel and embrace that idea, so we entered that process in earnest. Despite the hole I was in dealing with the complicated feelings and disappointment, this new project gave me something positive and forward looking to focus on. I found myself fired up once again by the idea of driving as much shareholder value as possible as my last and final project for this company that I had poured everything I had into.

We identified a representative to lead the process, drafted the memo (basically the proposal for the deal structure and finances), identified the top target companies, and messaged the plan to investors. While I'd been turning over this option for months, and came to the conclusion that it was the only path forward, communicating it with our investors and team was an impossibly hard update to write. When I hit send on the email, after reading and re-reading it for a week, it felt like we'd taken our first official step towards the end. I worried what people would think—despite training myself not to worry about others' feelings and knowing deep down we were making the right move—and I was scared shitless of the responses to that email.

They came in and were mostly positive.

"This is the craziest environment in start-ups I've ever seen, it's incredible you've kept CITYROW afloat for so long."

"This is definitely the right path, it will be very hard to raise future funds right now."

Some investors also pushed me with more questions and answers I didn't have yet like, "What does this mean for my investment?" and "What range do you expect the sale to be in?" and "Remind me where I sit and how much return do you think I'll have here?"

Memorializing the M&A plan into writing and sharing it with our supporters to me meant the end of our ten-year build. No matter what the outcome, we were going to start landing the plane and finding CITYROW a final resting place. It sounds like a death and in a lot of ways that was the level of grief I was experiencing over this period of time. I was grieving the loss of something big in my life, the loss of what could have been, the loss of a dream.

But a Merger and Acquisition it was.

And then the world had other plans.

Despite strong strategies and case study examples for how 1+1=5 in these acquisitions, when the deadline for final offers from companies that would potentially acquire us came, they were meager at best. Conversations that felt positive and where I left with high expectations just fell through. Each one was another dagger right into an open wound. I got excuse after excuse but at a macro level, so much of our industry was in shambles, no one had the bandwidth or capital to make a strong deal. We were left with one offer that was garbage (a joke on paper and honestly insulting) and one that might just *barely* be approved by the board.

When I went to the worst case scenario with friends, investors, and employees over the years—and more often in the past twelve months—never did I think this would be such a low blow in terms of a number that meant almost nothing to stakeholders—the people who had put their faith, and their money, in me over the last near-decade.

Nevertheless, it was the best option, so we persisted. It was summer and with a sixty-day timeline to close the deal, and barely enough money to support operations until then, we drove it in earnest.

While the deal moved in the background led by me, our CFO and an industry partner, Ashley and I struggled to find the right balance of communication to our remaining employees. Without the deal finalized and the forward plan for the integration still very up in the air, we had no idea who from our team the new company would want to bring with the deal and were not having any luck getting information from them. Our colleagues knew a deal was happening, and could feel the uncertainty from us, could see the pare back in production and the continuous cutting of expenses. It was a very challenging leadership position to be in, because there could be some optimistic future for the company, but we also wanted the people who'd stuck with us to protect their own career (and paycheck). It was shaky ground and kept us up at night.

In August we cut executive payroll. Ashley, our CFO Adam, and I would work without a salary and hope there would be a way to make it up post-close.

Even with this drastic move, our cash out date was six weeks away.

We pushed and pushed to get the deal moving and big questions about the transition answered but the potential acquirer's team was moving at a snails' pace.

With four weeks left, we had to make the tough call to let our last-standing team members go just after Labor Day.

In the final weeks together we set the rest of our content up for regular releases, prepped marketing emails and tied up as many loose ends with our team as we could.

Soon, it was just Ashley, Adam, myself, our lawyer, and our customer service rep left operating the business and keeping the company just barely afloat.

We'd meet every other day and pay the urgent payables to keep the company chugging along, we couldn't pay all of our outstanding bills but with recurring subscription revenue still hitting our bank regularly, we were able to stay just above $0 and managed to keep all of our creditors at bay.

Meanwhile, the deal was one step forward, two hundred steps back.

It was brutal. Not only were we confronting the worst fear of any founder, executive or board member, but the process was molasses.

We attempted to set deadlines for documents with the acquiring company only to hear, *"Thanks for your patience guys, we should have that to you next week."* We tried to get regular meetings on the calendar only to hear, *"Thanks for the touch base but let's regroup when we have something material next week."* It was obvious this was not a priority for their team, yet every time the company's principal got on the phone, he reiterated their commitment and enthusiasm for the deal.

Actions from their legal and execution team did not reflect that of the CEO and after sixty days, we still didn't have draft paperwork to review. This made us all question the long term viability that the deal would close. As they say, time kills all deals.

Not only that, they kept on coming back to renegotiate our signed Letter of Intent (LOI). Not minor points, but the biggest points of the deal. At one point we got on a call and the execution team told us that after six weeks of a signed LOI, they *"Don't see the value in the assets here and will be cutting the offer by a quarter. We did not review the deal room data so our apologies but can't see the full value we put in the original LOI."*

They kept pushing back until finally we had to say, "Ok fine, we'll go elsewhere."

They came back to the table and started moving things forward. It was clear they were playing games and we didn't have many of our own cards left to play.

But once again progress stalled. October first came and went and now Thanksgiving was approaching.

Never in our wildest dreams did we think this wouldn't be closed before Thanksgiving. From a business perspective, Ashley and I were banging our heads against the wall. There was so much opportunity to leverage this partnership for Black Friday and Cyber Monday and for holiday sales, as the fourth quarter is the biggest quarter for any consumer business. This fell on flat ears. Thanksgiving came and went.

At this point, it had been three months since payroll was cut.

As we attacked every opportunity to push the deal forward and ensure we were maximizing the value for creditors and shareholders, as the weeks and months dragged on, the fatigue set in.

During these months I lived in the gray area.

There was nothing else I could do to push the deal forward. I was doing my best to drive and shove and kick and scream things to move, but nothing budged.

Furthermore, I was personally out of gas. I had used up everything I had to push the M&A process on, and had a date in my mind that would finally close the door, on which I'd be able to open the next chapter—whatever that may be.

If I can only make it three more weeks, two more weeks… I kept telling myself.

But the end date kept moving. The door that I'd finally resolved to close wouldn't close, no matter how hard I pushed. At this point, all I wanted was to be on the other side and I couldn't get there. I was stuck.

A friend suggested the analogy that it was as if I had decided to get a divorce, but was still living with my ex. It resonated perfectly and that in-between, the gray area, the purgatory between two important things—whatever they may be—can be the hardest spots in anyone's life.

In the prior chapters of CITYROW, when we'd run out of money, when our partners let us down, when team members let me down, when a global pandemic smacked us upside down, we were down—but there was always an action plan to move forward. There was always a step to take, a decision to make, an email to send, a person to call and a to-do item to check off a list to move forward and solve even the biggest problems.

Now, there was no action to take. There was no future business to drive forward without a budget or team, there was just waiting, nudging and pushing as hard as possible without blowing the whole thing up. I'm a driver by nature and will move mountains to accomplish my goals. Here though, I had to be delicate. I was not the primary lead on the deal, it was our techpartner, and he had long-standing relationships that needed to be respected. I'm used to owning communication and pride myself on my ability to both communicate and manage big projects, and letting someone else do that (not nearly as well as I think I would have) was *painful*. It was one thing for the other side to make mistakes and not support the closing of the deal, but when I saw us not communicating perfectly or letting them walk over us in a way, it built on my already frustrated core. I wanted to take charge and drive this thing to completion—one way or another. And at this point, I was ready for the deal to fall apart if that's where it needed to go.

But a quick "No" is better than a long "Yes…"

… and for the sake of the team members left working for no pay and the dwindling bank account, we needed to know one way or another. I would have taken a firmer hand earlier on to figure this out but alas, I had to relinquish control.

In early summer, I had a call with my very first investor and constant mentor, Dan and he walked me through two of his recent acquisition stories. The theme he wanted me to take away was that they are, without fail, wild roller coasters. In each, the deal almost fell completely apart multiple times over. I listened carefully, pacing around my house, enjoying the stories but also feeling the second-hand stress. All of me hoping our story would be different.

Ours was exactly the same roller coaster, and then some.

The peaks and valleys were different and I was sure this deal would fall apart and we'd be forced into bankruptcy no less than eight times. I'd call Dan on the brink of tears and he'd remind me it's not over until it's over.

I continued to sit in purgatory and let the roller coaster ride continue.

Without anything to occupy me during this time and with nothing concrete to share with investors or our fractional employees one way or another, I faced a final challenge that I didn't see coming. Every day I wrestled with uncertainty and unknown and had to sit in that. For anyone who likes certainty and control (I think all of us?), there is no worse seat in life.

It dragged on and on and on until everyone on our side was beyond frustrated and ready to pull the plug entirely. CITYROW—down to the bare bones—was running out of time on the pre-programmed content and marketing we'd put in place over the summer, so it was now or never.

We'd get movement, then they'd stall. The only time to meet was Sunday nights (what kind of priority is that?!). Finally, we and WaterRower drew a firm line and made it clear the drop dead close date would be December twenty-second. Nothing like waiting until the last minute of the year...

This unlocked a closing plan and even though the acquiring company still didn't hit any deadlines (if paperwork was due on a Wednesday, it would come in on a Saturday, half uncompleted), and they even decided to try and re-negotiate for the fifteenth time in four months, at the final hour. But we held our ground and drove the pertinent documents forward. Still, the last business day of the year came and went and they asked us for a legal call on Christmas Eve; everyone dropped everything to get the final documents ready and submitted for execution. Then came a week of holidays, and soon it was the first week of the new year.

Now they were back to the same antics, and now our clients were starting to feel it. They noticed the lack of content, they questioned what was going to happen to CITYROW and their business and retention was at risk with each day—each minute—that went by.

A closing call was finally set for the third week of January and our partner who facilitated the deal was onsite. I was on a coaching call the hour before the call with a young founder, helping them set up their investor relations cadence, working on the KPI's for their business, excited about what lay ahead for them and knowing I'd be a strong partner through the ups and the downs for them. At that moment, our internal deal text pinged: "They are pulling out of the deal."

I was unable to process, but my first instinct was that they were playing yet another game with us and I was fed up. Quickly it became real and an hour later when we hopped on the phone, they confirmed that [for no good reason], they were pulling out of the deal. This was ludicrous. Totally fine to pull out in September, October…but January? Business is ruthless but I still and will always believe in acting in integrity—this clearly was poor business ethics.

After six months—with nothing left in the back account or any kind of physical or emotional tank for myself or anyone at CITYROW, we were back at square 1, and this time with many less subscribers and an urgent need to get more content out to our clients. I didn't have time to process the shock, but at the same time, I knew in my gut that we'd just dodged a huge bullet. No matter if it was the best deal we could've gotten; no way I wanted our brand and clients to end up in the wrong hands.

The day after, and a few rounds of crying big tears, I got a call from my CFO, who had spoken to WaterRower—miraculously, they would step into similar economics of the deal that fell through and move quickly to seal it.

All of a sudden I felt lighter, the unease I had with the prior potential owner was gone and I knew this was how the story was meant to end. WaterRower was our partner of over a decade and there were so many synergies in our businesses, it made all the sense in the world for this to be how and where the CITYROW story ended.

On Valentine Day 2024, 10 years to the day of my back surgery, that I wrote all about in the first chapter of this book, we signed paperwork to have WaterRower acquire CITYROW.

The finality and specificity of closing on this ten-year anniversary is not lost on me.

❧

Fighting tooth and nail until the final breath, far past when there was payroll, when there were only four people working part-time without pay to see the final chapter through. CITYROW ultimately found its home within a larger company, and I got us there.

The ending is not pretty. It's sad. It's disappointing.

I'm pissed. We should have won. The strategy we pioneered—which was rock solid, but just didn't fit into anyone's thesis because it straddled brick and mortar and digital—will be what every company does from here on out: it's the future of our industry. We had it, we were so close, then it was ripped away.

I will always think about the what if's…what if COVID hadn't happened…what if we were able to launch our best franchise studios that spring with the next ten following that year? What if digital growth was even paced to reflect the naturally growing demand? What if everyone and every dollar hadn't raced into our market to try and make a buck?

The process for finding the final resting place for CITYROW was made harder because of these factors, because every potential partner faced the same industry economics. We were hopeful when we started the process that we'd find a decent home for a decent financial outcome. By the middle, we were just hoping for a solid ending. In the last weeks, the verdict was out on what was going to happen and I wasn't sure there was much left to fight for.

I struggled hard during this process, having to let our investors down, the top ones personally, one by one, in emotional and hard conversations. I had to let our team down. I had to process my own disappointment and anger. There would be little to show on paper at the end of the ten-year build. We had done so much, nurtured and grew such an incredible community and product, and on paper it would be a failure. There's no sugar-coating that. It's a fact.

Personally, this rocked me to my core. I pride myself on being someone who delivers, who lives in integrity and who makes commitments and keeps them. These final moments put me in a position where I had to face the facts that are the opposite of what I stand for.

I'm going to be mad for a while, but I'm also able to hold immense gratitude for the experience.

It's impossible to put into words what these ten years did to a young entrepreneur. They groomed me, they built me, they challenged me and they shaped me. It was my MBA, it was start-up boot camp, it was my fake law degree in securities. It was the adventure of a lifetime and I did it alongside two of my best friends— who are still my best friends after ten years of this journey.

What's next? I'm not sure. Maybe I'll take a break from being the CEO/quarterback and embrace my love of coaching and helping early start-ups. I love being the person for others that I could have only dreamed of for myself in my early days. I'll think about getting my hands dirty again and starting or building alongside incredible people. I also need to carve the time and space for myself to process and recover from this ten-year push.

I'm taking so much from these ten years—I'm both excited and nervous to see where best to apply myself in this next chapter.

Being a founder is a lonely game (and sometimes I made it more lonely than it had to be by keeping everything—including my emotions—close to my chest at times) and learned along the way that leaning on people and finding your tribe requires a lot of vulnerability, but is also the biggest unlock to doing and achieving more.

So few people have walked this founder path and if I could share this CITYROW story with young Helaine, she (and probably everyone around her) would be shocked to hear that this was the path she'd walk on. Despite knowing the pain throughout and the ultimate ending, I'd tell her to do it, to jump in, that the water is cold and full of sea creatures but to jump in anyway. I'd also tell her to find her tribe, lean on fellow founders and former founders, find a handful of people who you can trust and let them be a part of the story.

This is not your typical hero's journey. This isn't a rainbows and butterflies fairytale. This is the real, raw and gritty story that is unfortunately more like the untold stories of most founders. So if you choose this path, admire this path or are in some way a part of this path, know you're not alone in the loneliness, the heartbreak and the true insanity it takes to embark on this start-up journey.

EPILOGUE
THE JOY IN THE JOURNEY

One Thanksgiving many years ago, my grandma found some cute little dishes with sayings on them and passed them out to our family as gifts. We all got one with a different quote. At first, I rolled my eyes—it was incredibly on-brand for my family to get deep on Thanksgiving. I braced myself for a big discussion about everyone's plates and what their sayings meant to them.

My dish said, "Joy is the journey."

I did not immediately realize the power of the words, but I used it as a small jewelry dish happily having it remind me of my grandma every time I did. Over time, I would look at it and process its meaning—the phrase could not have been truer about CITYROW—and me.

"Joy is the journey" means celebrating wins and recognizing milestones, no matter how seemingly small. It means calling them out, and taking the time and space to pause and recognize them.

Founders are never satisfied, never done, and never happy. There's always more to do, but you must stop and celebrate how far you've come—as people and as builders. I'm so grateful that I (and the team) did this regularly.

I remember the day we signed the term sheet for the Series A. It was such a big deal and I was overwhelmed with both what we'd just accomplished but already thinking about what lay ahead. The official signing was the thing that I've been thinking about for so long, tactically negotiating and waiting on for weeks, so by the time it was signed, it felt anticlimactic. I was home alone on a hot summer night in my Williamsburg apartment when the last documents were sent. I was bone tired, but still, knew I had to celebrate it in some small way. This was a big fucking deal, even if all I felt was fatigue. So I took myself to the Van Lewen ice cream shop for a decadent frozen dinner—with rainbow sprinkles.

A few weeks later, when we finally closed the round, when the money was in the bank, and before the *TechCrunch* announcement came out, I knew we had to celebrate this milestone as a team as well. The ice cream was for me, but the team was equally as important, and we needed to take a pause and celebrate. I was rushing ahead, already worried about execution and itching to get to work, but I knew we had to appreciate and recognize this milestone in a big way. The next week we all gathered for drinks, dinner and shuffleboard to toast the milestone. Whatever would unfold next would unfold, but this was a seven-year goal we'd just accomplished, and that is *something*.

It's vulnerable, and almost sad to me to admit this, but I had met enough founders before and during the CITYROW story to know (even though I didn't want to believe it) that deep down there might be a day where I resented—or even hated—CITYROW.

That's a crazy thought from someone who spent an entire decade building and nurturing it.

This is unfortunately based on real data (the reality is, most—upwards of 90 percent—of start-ups fail) and so many founders that I knew had one of three outcomes, all of which felt shitty in some way to me.

1. They grew the business, it was wildly successful, they sold it or IPO'd. And it became so far from the thing that they started that it no longer brought them joy in the same way. (Okay, of course this is a desired outcome. It is relatively awesome, but it can still lead to resentment and drama.)

2. It was an acqui-hire, which a huge percentage of companies and founders go through upon being acquired, and the founder worked for the new company now. Maybe they made some money, maybe they didn't, and they process their own feelings about the outcome, plus work for someone else.

3. Something else happened and they had to shut the business down.

So, like in life, I'm grateful I had the foresight to really enjoy the journey while driving toward our big goal. It's not [all] about the destination because the destination could be epic, but it is almost always something you had never imagined or seen coming. Just as I'm glad we celebrated that Series A in a big way, I'm glad we took the time for team lunches, dinners, and picking out new "CITYROW Crew" sweatshirts to give to team members every holiday. I'm glad we took a day off every summer to play kickball (go Blue Crew!) and that Annie and Ashley and I had a bougie dinner at a French restaurant when we got the Series A money in. I'm glad that we went to dinner to celebrate with our franchisees when we opened a new location. I'm glad that we woke up early and had mimosas together on the day the *Today* show aired. I'm glad I took myself for that ice cream dinner.

It's really, really hard for founders to celebrate something that isn't the ultimate goal or for most of us in life to celebrate the little wins along the way when we maybe think there's so much more around the corner. We feel like the work is never done. There's always so much more. We're overachievers. We're perfectionists. We're idea-generators. We want 15,000 more projects. We're two years ahead on the roadmap in our head. We never think anything is good enough so it's extra hard for us to see that success along the way and enjoy the journey. But we must remember the joy in the journey, in both business and in life.

There is always going to be the adventure and the small wins. Sure, you strive toward the golden ticket, but if you don't enjoy the journey, you may never enjoy a single second until it's too late.

And the destination, the finish line—regardless of what you envision it being—is likely not the destination at all, it's just another beginning.

WHAT'S NEXT?

I want YOU to jump in!...and I want to help.

First off, for book resources and more (maybe a gift!) go here: helaineknapp.com/making-waves-resources.

No matter what you're facing, there is a specific way of thinking in order to best and most successfully navigate it. I've put together resources, webinars and .pdfs with some frameworks that apply to any stage of life or business to help you jump in and prepare to solve whatever lies ahead.

Whether it's for a business idea, big personal decision or company transformation, here's how to connect with me:

1:1 Coaching: This one is my favorite. Tell me what you're building. Bring me a problem. Let's solve it together 1x1 with pre-scheduled time (book on my website) and I promise we'll find some unique solutions and carve out a strong path forward.

Advisor: Need regular, ongoing support getting through this phase and probably the next? Need someone to bat ideas around with and make a plan? There are always more cards to play, let's find them. I provide support, direction and confidence to anything from business strategy, investor relations, people challenges and any and all unique problems that early to mid-sized companies face.

Consulting: Have a big project without the right executor? I'll engage directly on a short to mid-term project having a direct impact on your trajectory. This includes, but isn't limited to, fundraising strategy, sales strategy, and overall company growth strategy and planning.

Speaking: Need to engage and inspire a larger group? I have been a featured speaker on all things business growth, entrepreneurship, wellness and fitness, fundraising, and trends around each of these areas.

Small-Group Solving: Want to problem solve in a small group format with other like-minded builders? Join a workshop and work through not just your challenge but witness the problem solving of others around you. This format is magical and not only do you personally reap the benefits from a path forward, but forge relationships and camaraderie that can be that support system for you in the long run.

Investing: Have a new great idea or are on the brink of building something? As an angel investor and overall connector, I want to bet on the founder who's never going to give up...because as you know, I am that person, too.

Let's have some fun navigating what's next.

Learn more at www.helaineknapp.com.

ACKNOWLEDGMENTS

What a crazy journey this has been to write and develop this book. To even begin to understand my deep gratitude and thanks, I must start with two stories. The first is a blind email I received from a literary agent the day after I appeared on the Today Show back in 2018. During that time I received a crazy amount of inbounds and most of them were nothing material but this email was from a book agent who urged me to write a book. Curiosity got the best of me so we had a call or two and left it to potentially something in the future.

Fast forward to the early days of COVID, when I was speaking with a former colleague, friend, author and fellow female founder who multiple times over our tenure collaborating would say, "When are we going to write your book?"

Without social engagements, time was plenty and it was finally time to dig in, compile the stories, themes, learnings and do the deep hard work to get this book ready for primetime. Leanne Shear, thank you for the initial push(es) and ongoing support, collaboration and belief in me and this project. You saw this vision even before I did. I joke this was all your idea and all your fault, but I stand by that!

When Leanne and I were ready with a rough proposal and sample chapters, we called that literary agent I had flagged in my inbox. After a few calls it was clear that Erin Niumata at Folio Lit also saw this potential in this story (since 2018!) and was going to be the right person to see this vision through. Over the next two years, over many iterations of what this book could or would be and throughout some of the toughest mountains and steepest valleys of CITYROW, both Leanne and Erin carried this project through towards the vision that Debby Englander and Post Hill saw the promise in.

There are so many people to thank that made this book possible but it would not have even been a project without the two women that sat at the helm of CITYROW with me since day one. Ashley and Annie, words can't describe how grateful I am for us... and our adventure of a lifetime. We gave it all we had and then when we didn't think there was more to give, we found it. We went far, together, and despite the ending, I love our story.

To our CITYROW crew wide and far, thank you for believing in us, our vision, our journey and our product. Thank you for trusting us with your bodies, your energy and your resources. Thank you for encouraging us with your sweaty selfies and dedication to classes both at home and in studios nationwide.

I'd like to thank my incredible family for indulging in many early interviews to help extract a bit more about early Helaine that even I didn't remember; my college friends for helping me recall some of the best and worst days of college life; my close friends and family for taking early reads of the manuscript, listening to me vent about the process, and encouraging me to be proud and keep going even when things were challenging in the last few years.

The amount of encouragement I felt throughout the ten year CITYROW journey took a village and I am eternally grateful for the mentors, investors and advisors—both formal and informal—that helped guide me and CITYROW through all the twists and turns.

My support system is everything and I would not be the strong woman I am today without the urgent pep talks, extra hugs and deep love and support they have shown me as a constant throughout all the storms.

Thank you to: Adam Devine, Adam Mizel, Adam Wilks, Adrian Morante, Alex Spiro, Ali Peikon, Amir Hazan, Amy Mitrani, Amy Sullivan, Annie Mulgrew, Arie Abecassis, Ariel Toback, Ashley Davis Keith, Ashley Locke, Benjamin Lurie, Beth Lewis, Bonnie Bergstein, Brock Emmetsberger, Chad Bronstein, Dan Reich, Dan Schneider, Danielle Kantor, Danielle Wieder, Dave Keil, David Barr, David Jones, Dhani Jones, Edward Sullivan, Fred Knapp, Ian Burnstein, Ilana Brown, Isaiah Toback, Jared Finklestein, Jared Spiegel, Jason Klarreich, Jeff Keeler, Jeff Ragovin, Jen Bassuk, Jenny Fielding, Jessica Aris, Jim Fendt, Joel Wish, John Rotche, Jonathan Drennan, Jonathan Keith, Josh Knapp, Kass Lazerow, Kat Cole, Katelyn Cannella, Katelyn Kiernan, Kelly Mullane, Kim Kaupe, Kristin Weitzel, Kurt Giehl, Laura Markofsky, Laurel Shipley, Lauren Burbank, Mariel Bronen, Michele Laven, Mike Nikolai, Mohammed Iqbal, Najeeb Ahmad, Nicole Tiberia, Noah Heller, Patrick Finnegan, Pau Sabria, Paula Lustbader, Petamber Pahuja, Peter King, Peter Ehrlich, Rebecca Abramson Rick Caro, Rob Crocker, Sharon Fox, Siobhan Houlihan, Steph Bagley, Steven Abramson, Susan Mitrani Knapp, Tom Bergman, Vanessa Edwards.

Lastly, to the founders who have jumped in or are thinking about jumping in.

Your wave is waiting. Chase it. Ride it. Find your tribe. Make it yours.

And don't hesitate to reach out and tell me about it: Helaine@ HelaineKnapp.com.

With warmth and solidarity,

Helaine

ABOUT THE AUTHOR

 Helaine is the Founder & CEO of CITYROW, well renowned speaker, investor, advisor and industry leader.

While hustling start-ups in NYC in the early 2010's Helaine fell hard for group fitness classes. A lower back injury forced her to find a workout that was low impact, but super effective. After a friend suggested rowing, Helaine initially rejected it as something "my dad did in college," but following a few workouts and pairing it with strength work changed her mind and the concept for CITYROW was born.

Under Knapp's leadership, with a mission of delivering a smart, fun, and effective workout to all fitness levels, CITYROW grew from one studio in New York City to a national fitness brand featuring at-home rowers, premium streaming content and a nation-wide franchise system.

Knapp is sought after for media and has been featured on *TODAY*, *Women's Health*, *ABC*, *Harper's Bazaar*, *Shape*, *Well + Good*, *Vogue*, *Yahoo! Finance* and *PEOPLE*, among many others.

www.helaineknapp.com for more information